Famous
Men of Greece

by

John Haaren

Published by
Feather Trail Press

Table of Contents

Preface

The study of history, like the study of a landscape, should begin with the most conspicuous features. Not until these have been fixed in memory will the lesser features fall into their appropriate places and assume their right proportions.

The famous men of ancient and modern times are the mountain peaks of history. It is logical then that the study of history should begin with the biographies of these men.

Not only is it logical; it is also pedagogical. Experience has proven that in order to attract and hold the child's attention each conspicuous feature of history presented to him should have an individual for its center. The child identifies himself with the personage presented. It is not Romulus or Hercules or Cæsar or Alexander that the child has in mind when he reads, but himself, acting under similar conditions.

Prominent educators, appreciating these truths, have long recognized the value of biography as a preparation for the study of history and have given it an important place in their scheme of studies.

The former practice in many elementary schools of beginning the detailed study of American history without any previous knowledge of general history limited the pupil's range of vision, restricted his sympathies, and left him without material for comparisons. Moreover, it denied to him a knowledge of his inheritance from the Greek philosopher, the Roman lawgiver, the Teutonic lover of freedom. Hence the recommendation so strongly urged in the report of the Committee of Ten—and emphasized, also, in the report of the Committee of Fifteen—that the study of Greek, Roman and modern European history in the form of biography should precede the study of detailed American history in our elementary schools. The Committee of Ten recommends an eight years' course in history, beginning with the fifth year in school and continuing to the end of the high school course. The first two years of this course are given wholly to the study of biography and mythology. The Committee of Fifteen recommends that history be taught in all the grades of the elementary school and emphasizes the value of biography and of general history.

The series of historical stories to which this volume belongs was prepared in conformity with the foregoing recommendations and with the best practice of leading schools. It has been the aim of the authors to make an interesting story of each man's life and to tell those stories in a style so simple that pupils in the lower grades will read them with pleasure, and so dignified that they may be used with profit as text-books for reading.

Teachers who find it impracticable to give to the study of mythology and biography a place of its own in an already overcrowded curriculum usually prefer to correlate history with reading and for this purpose the volumes of this series will be found most desirable.

The value of the illustrations can scarcely be over-estimated. They will be found to surpass in number and excellence anything heretofore offered in a school-book. For the most part they are reproductions of world-famous pictures, and for that reason the artists' names are generally affixed.

NEPTUNE AND HIS HORSES

Chapter 1

The Gods of Greece

PART I

IN the southern part of Europe is a little country called Greece. It is the home of a nation called the Greeks, and Greeks have lived in it for more than three thousand years. In olden times they believed that before they came to the land it was the home of the gods, and they used to tell wonderful stories of what happened when the gods lived in the country. One of these stories was about a god called Cronos, and his children.

Cronos was the first king of the gods. He had a wife named Rhea. His mother told him that one of his children would take his kingdom from him. He determined that this should never happen, and so he swallowed his children as soon as they were born. His cruelty distressed Rhea very much, and when a sixth child was born she made a plan to save its life. She gave Cronos a stone wrapped in baby-clothes, and this he swallowed.

Then Rhea took the child and hid him in a cave. And though the cave was dark he filled it with bright light; so she named him Zeus, which means brightness. We call him Jupiter.

Jupiter had one of the strangest nurses that a baby ever had. It was a goat. However, she took such good care of him that when she died she was changed into a group of stars, which shine in the sky to this day.

When Jupiter grew up he went to war against his cruel father. Cronos persuaded some giants, called Titans, to help him in fighting Jupiter. These Titans were so strong that they pulled up hills and mountains and threw them at Jupiter as easily as boys throw snowballs at one another. Jupiter soon saw that he must find some match for the Titans. So he asked another family of giants to aid him. They were called Cyclops, or Round-Eye, because each had only one eye, which was round and was in the middle of his forehead. The Cyclops were famous blacksmiths, and they made thunder and lightning for Jupiter. So when the Titans hurled mountains, Jupiter hurled back bolts of thunder and flashes of lightning. The battle was a terrible one. Jupiter was the victor.

After this great battle Jupiter made Cronos bring back to life the children whom he had swallowed, and then he gave to each of his brothers and sisters a part of the kingdom of their wicked father. He made himself the king of the gods, and for his own kingdom he took the blue sky. He made his sister Here, whom we call Juno, the goddess of the clouds and queen of all the gods.

To his brother Poseidon, whom we call Neptune, he gave the ocean, and he made his brother Hades, whom we call Pluto, king of the regions under the earth and sea.

He made his sister Demeter, whom we call Ceres, queen of the grains, the fruits and the flowers.

His sister Hestia, whom we call Vesta, he made the goddess of fire and gave her charge of the homes and hearthstones of men.

PART II

WHEN the kingdom of Cronos had been divided, the new rulers found a great deal to do. In the depths of the sea Neptune built a palace whose floor was of snow-white shells and blood-red coral, while the walls were of shining mother-of-pearl. When the waves above his palace were wild, Neptune would yoke his brazen-hoofed horses to his chariot and, standing with his trident, or three-pronged spear, in his hand, would drive swiftly over the water. And as the brazen hoofs of the horses trampled upon the waves the sea became calm.

The underground world of Pluto was a dreary region. It was the home of the dead. Round it flowed a black river called the "Styx," or "Hateful." The only way to cross this river was in a ferryboat rowed by a silent boatman named Charon. At the gateway of the under world was the terrible watch-dog Kerberus, or, as we spell the name, Cerberus. When the old Greeks buried a person they put a coin in his mouth and a barley-cake sweetened with honey in his hand. The coin was to pay Charon for taking the spirit across the Styx and the cake was to be thrown to Cerberus, so that, while he was eating it, the spirit might pass unnoticed into the spirit-land.

PLUTO AND CERBERUS

No goddess was willing to be Pluto's wife and live in his world of gloom. So he was very lonely. One day he visited the upper world in his chariot drawn by four handsome coal-black steeds. He saw a beautiful maiden, named Persephone, whom we call Proserpine, gathering flowers in a meadow. Pluto at once bore her off to his kingdom of darkness and married her. Thus she became the queen of the lower world.

This made life much pleasanter for Pluto, but it was very hard for Proserpine. She loved sunshine and flowers, and she grieved for them so much that at last Jupiter took pity upon her and persuaded Pluto to let her come back to the land of light for a part of every year. When she made her yearly visits, the flowers that she loved so dearly bloomed for her, the grass grew green, and it was spring. When the time came that she must return to Pluto, all the flowers drooped and died, the grass turned brown, and bleak winter followed.

PLUTO CARRYING OFF PROSERPINE

The sisters of Jupiter had a great deal to do in their fair kingdoms. Every spring and summer Ceres caused the different kinds of fruits and grains and flowers to grow. As she could not do all this work alone she had thousands of beautiful maidens, called nymphs, to help her. There was a wood-nymph in every tree to make its leaves green and glossy and to color its blossoms. There was a water-nymph in every spring that bubbled out of the hills, and one in every stream that flowed through the valleys. The nymphs of the springs and brooks watered the plants and crops of Ceres and made them grow.

Vesta was the sister to whom had been given charge of the home and hearthstone. She caused the fires to glow, which burned on the hearth and made home cheery and gave warmth to the family and to strangers who came to see them. In every city and town of Greece a fire sacred to Vesta was always kept burning.

PART III

In his kingdom of the sky Jupiter dwelt in splendor, but he was not always happy; for although Juno, his queen, was a lovely in face and form, she was more beautiful than good-tempered; and sometimes she and Jupiter had bitter quarrels.

One of the sons of Jupiter was named Hermes or Mercury. He wore golden sandals and

JUPITER AND JUNO

carried a wonderful wand. On the heels of the sandals were wings with which he could fly through the air like a bird. Because he could travel so swiftly he became the messenger of the gods.

Another son of Jupiter was Hephaestus, whom we call Vulcan. He was the god of fire and the friend of workers in metals. He had a great forge under Mount Ætna, and there he made wonderful things of iron and brass. The round-eyed Cyclops were his blacksmiths. One day Vulcan was rude to his father, who to punish him hurled him from heaven. Vulcan fell upon rocks and broke his leg and ever after that was lame.

Ares, the terrible god of war, whom we call Mars, was another son of Jupiter. He delighted in battle and bloodshed.

MINERVA

Apollo and his twin sister Artemis, or Diana, were also children of Jupiter. They were both beautiful. Apollo's beauty was so great that when we wish to say that a man is handsome in face and form, we say, "He is an Apollo." Apollo and Diana were great favorites with Jupiter, who made Apollo the god of the sun, and Diana the goddess of the moon. To each he gave a silver bow, from which they shot arrows of light.

The most wonderful daughter of Jupiter was Athene, whom we usually call Minerva. One day the king of the gods had a headache from which he could get no relief; so he sent for Vulcan. When the great blacksmith arrived at his father's palace Jupiter said to him, "Split open my head with your axe." As soon as Vulcan had done this, a maiden goddess, clothed in armor, sprang from the head of Jupiter. The maiden was Minerva, the goddess of wisdom.

9

PART IV

Most beautiful of all the goddesses was Aphrodite, or Venus, who sprang from the foam of the sea. She was the goddess of love. Several of the gods wished to marry her. Jupiter decided the matter strangely by giving her to Vulcan, the ugliest of all the gods.

Venus had a son named Eros, or Cupid, the god of love. He carried a bow and arrows, and if one of his arrows pierced the heart of a mortal, that mortal fell in love.

JUNO, CUPID, and VENUS

There was a fair goddess named Iris, who caused the rainbow to brighten dark storm-clouds, and often bore messages from heaven to men.

There were also many other gods and goddesses. Three sisters were known as the Graces. They made mortals gracious and lovable, friendly and pleasant in their ways.

There were three other sisters called the Furies. Their forms were draped in black, and their hair was twined with serpents. They punished wicked people and gave them no peace as long as they lived.

Higher than all gods and goddesses were three weird sisters, called the Fates. Not even Jupiter could change the plans of the Fates. Whatever they said must come to pass always happened. Whatever they said should not happen never took place. When a child was born, one of the sisters began to spin the thread of its life. The second decided how long the thread should be. The third cut the thread when the moment came for the life to end.

After men came to Greece and dwelt there the gods and goddesses withdrew to the far-away peaks of Olympus, the highest mountain in Greece, and made their home there.

Chapter 2

Deucalion and the Flood

UPON Olympus there was for every god a shining palace of brass, built by Vulcan and the Cyclops; and every day the gods gathered in the great banqueting hall of Jupiter to feast upon ambrosia and drink nectar from goblets of gold.

APOLLO AND THE MUSES

At the banquets they were served by a lovely maiden named Hebe, who was the goddess of youth. While they feasted Apollo played on his lyre and the Muses sang. The muses were the nine goddesses of poetry, arts, and sciences. Even in our own language playing and singing are called "music" in memory of them.

Sometimes the gods came down from Olympus to visit the men in Greece and taught them what we call the "useful arts." Minerva, the goddess of wisdom, showed them how to harness horses and plow the ground. She showed the women how to spin and weave.

Ceres, the great earth-mother who made the fields fruitful, showed the farmers how to sow wheat and barley. Then, when the grain was ripe, she taught the farmers' wives how to make bread.

Vulcan taught the Greeks how to make plows, spades and hoes and many other things of iron and brass.

When the gods came down now and then from Olympus they found that the early Greeks were very wicked. The kindness of the gods made them no better; so at last Jupiter decided to destroy them by a flood.

A certain half-god, half man, named Prometheus, or Forethought, warned the Greeks of their danger. The only person that heeded his warning was his own son, Deucalion. With Pyrrha, his wife, Deucalion got into an ark as soon as the rain began.

It rained all over Greece for days and days. The rivers and brooks overflowed. The valleys were filled. The trees disappeared. All but the highest mountains were covered. But Deucalion's ark rode safely. At last the rain ceased. For nine days the ark drifted about on the face of the water. Then it grounded.

When the waters had gone down somewhat, Deucalion and Pyrrha found that they were on one of the mountains of Greece, called Parnassus. They left their ark and walked down the mountain. Of all the Greeks only these two were left; and among the quiet hills and valleys near or far not a living creature was to be seen. The loneliness made them fearful. Scarcely knowing whither they went, they came suddenly upon a deep cleft in the rocks. Out of the cleft dense volumes of steam and gas were pouring. Deucalion, who was braver than his wife, peered into the cleft; and while he did so, a wonderful voice came from the depths.

It said, "Cast behind you the bones of your mother!"

"An oracle!" cried Pyrrha.

"An oracle it is!" Deucalion cried.

Long ages before the flood, the gods used some times to speak with men and give them advice about things that were going to happen. What they said was called an "oracle," a word that means something told by the gods to men.

So now Deucalion and Pyrrha felt sure that one of the gods was telling them something.

But they wondered what the words "Cast behind you the bones of your mother" could mean. After a while Deucalion said:

"Pyrrha, the earth is our mother."

"Very true," said she.

"Then," cried Deucalion, "the bones of our mother must be the stones of the earth."

Both now saw plainly that the oracle meant that they should cast behind them the stones that lay scattered upon the ground. So they went on down the mountain, and as they went they picked up stones which they cast behind them.

Soon they heard the clatter of many feet behind them, and looking back they saw that the stones which Deucalion had thrown had turned into a troop of young men, who were following Deucalion, while the stones that Pyrrha had thrown had become a band of girls, who were following Pyrrha.

HOUSEHOLD ART
OF THE EARLY GREEKS

Deucalion and Pyrrha were no longer lonely; and they had plenty to do for they taught the youths and maidens the arts of plowing and spinning and weaving that they themselves had learned from the gods before the flood.

Stones lay thick on the face of the land, and the hills were covered with forests. With the stones walls were made, and with timber from the forest roofs and floors were laid, and thus houses were built. Farms were then laid out, fields were sown, and vines and olive trees planted. Soon the valley below Mount Parnassus was crowded with many people. In time the race of Deucalion and Pyrrha spread from valley to valley, up and down the land of Greece.

The people called themselves Hellenes, because one of the sons of Deucalion was named Hellen. Their country, which, as you have learned, we call Greece, they called Hellas.

Chapter 3

Cadmus and the Dragon's Teeth

IN a land of Asia, named Phœnicia, lived King Agenor with his queen. They had four children—three sons and a beautiful daughter named Europa.

One morning, as the young people were playing in a meadow near the seashore, a snow-white bull came toward them. Europa and her brothers thought it would be a fine frolic to take a ride on the back of the bull; and the brothers agreed that Europa should have the first ride. In a moment she was on the bull's back, and the bull was capering over the meadow. Then, suddenly, he ran down to the shore and plunged into the sea. For a little while he could be seen swimming through the water, with Europa clinging to his horns. Then both disappeared, and Europa never saw her brothers or her father or her mother again. Still, her fate was not a sad one. At the end of a long ride on the back of the bull she reached that part of the world which to this day is called Europe in her honor. There she married a king, and was queen for all the rest of her life.

EUROPA ON THE BULL'S BACK

But in her old home there was great distress. Agenor sent his sons to look for her and told them not to return until they had found their sister. Their mother went with them. After a long time the two elder sons gave up the search and settled in a strange land. The mother and the youngest son, Cadmus, wandered on until her death. With her last breath she made him promise to go to Mount Parnassus and ask the oracle where he might find Europa. As soon as she was dead Cadmus made haste to Parnassus. When he arrived at the mountain, he found the cleft in the rocks from which long before the oracle had come to Deucalion. Cadmus stood before the stream of gas which poured from it and asked for advice.

From the cleft came a deep roaring sound. Then he heard the puzzling words, "Follow the cow; and build a city where she lies down."

Cadmus saw a cow nibbling tufts of grass by the roadside, not far from where he was standing. He decided to follow her and, with some companions, set out on his unknown journey.

For a long time it seemed as though the cow would not lie down at all, but, finally, she began to double her knees under her, as cows do, and in a second more she was at rest on the ground. Cadmus and his men decided to camp on the spot for the night. They looked about for some water and found a spring bubbling out from under a rock.

Now this was really an enchanted spring. It was guarded by a dragon that had the claws of a lion, the wings of an eagle and the jaws of a serpent. When Cadmus and his men came near, the dragon sprang from behind the rock and killed all but Cadmus.

Luckily, Cadmus had his sword with him, and so, when the dragon, with wide-open jaws, flew at him, he thrust his sword down the fiery throat and into the creature's heart. The monster fell dead, and through the air rang the words, "Sow the teeth of the dragon, O Cadmus!"

Though he saw that it would be hard work to break the great teeth out of the dragon's jaws, Cadmus at once set about the task, When it was finished, he dug the soil with the point of his sword as best he could and planted half of the monster's teeth.

Never had grown such a wonderful crop. For every tooth that was planted a warrior, armed and eager to fight, sprang up. Cadmus gazed in amazement, until a voice in the air commanded, "Throw a stone among the warriors."

Cadmus obeyed, and immediately every warrior drew his sword and attacked one of his companions. The woods rang with the din of the battle. One by one the warriors fell, until only five were left. Cadmus now shouted loudly to them, "Be at peace!" When they stopped fighting, he added, "Building is better than killing." And every man of the five immediately repeated the words, "Building is better than killing."

"Then let us build a city here!" cried Cadmus; for they were standing where the cow had lain down.

The warriors agreed, and all set to work to build a city. They called the city Thebes; and in later days it became very famous.

The land around Thebes was rich and covered with grass. So Cadmus and his friends raised cattle. But there were many robbers in Greece, who often made raids upon the cattle and stole some of the finest animals.

For protection against the robbers a wall was built. It was not a wall laid by masons, but a magic wall built by a strange musician called Amphion. He struck such sweet music from his lyre that the stones danced about and took their proper places in the wall.

When Cadmus was a boy at his father's palace in Phœnicia, he and his brothers and the lost Europa had been taught to read and write; and now that peace and plenty filled his land, he determined to teach his people the arts of reading and writing. So the men of Thebes learned their a-b-c's, and Cadmus' school was the first in Europe where people were taught to read.

But Cadmus was not happy. He was condemned to eight years of punishment for killing the dragon. After the punishment was over, Jupiter gave him Harmony, the daughter of Venus, for a wife, and all the gods came to the wedding feast. One of the wedding presents was a necklace that brought bad luck to any one who wore it, and Harmony had great misfortunes. Bowed with grief, she and Cadmus left Thebes and settled in the western part of Greece. Finally, Jupiter pitied them in their trouble, turned them into serpents, and carried them to the realm of the blessed.

Chapter 4

Perseus

PART I

IN a Grecian city named Argos lived beautiful Danaë, the king's daughter. An oracle warned the king that he would be killed by Danaë's son. To save his life he ordered Danaë and her child, Perseus, to be shut up in a chest and cast adrift on the Mediterranean Sea.

PERSEUS

For two days and nights the chest floated on the water. At the end of that time it struck against some rocks on the shore of an island called Seriphos. There was a little opening in the side of the chest, and peeping through it, Danaë saw a man coming over the rocks toward her. As soon as he was near enough, he threw a fishing net over the chest and drew it ashore.

He broke the chest open and let Danaë out. Then he told her that she had landed upon an island ruled by his brother, Polydectes. His own name was Dictys. He took Danaë and her child to his home.

Years went by, and Perseus grew to be a strong and handsome man. Danaë was still a beautiful woman and Polydectes fell in love with her. She refused his love, and Perseus also was unwilling that he should marry her. Then Polydectes told Perseus that he was about to marry, and that he wished to give the head of the Gorgon, Medusa, to his bride for a present. Perseus promised to get him the Gorgon's head. This pleased Polydectes. He did not want the Gorgon's head, but he asked for it because he believed that the young man would never return alive if he went in search of it.

The Gorgons were three horrible sisters who lived on a distant island near the land of the setting sun. Their hair was snakes that hissed at all who came near them. They had wings of gold and claws of brass. Two of them were immortal, but the youngest, Medusa, was mortal. Her face was that of a beautiful woman, but never free from a frown; and whoever looked upon it was turned to stone.

When Perseus had made his promise, he went out from the palace and sat on the cliffs of Seriphos. While he was gazing at the white-capped sea, Mercury, the messenger of the gods, appeared before him and promised help from himself and from Minerva, the goddess of wisdom. Minerva would lend her shield, Mercury offered his sword of light, and both agreed to guide him to the land of the setting sun, where the three Gray Sisters lived. These sisters would tell him the way to the home of the Hesperides. The Hesperides were beautiful nymphs who had three magic treasures, which Perseus must get before he could reach the land of the Gorgons.

Leaving Seriphos, Perseus began his long journey to the land of the setting sun. When he arrived there he found the three Gray Sisters. They were the strangest beings that he had ever seen. They had among them only one eye and one tooth, which they passed in turn from one to another.

PERSEUS AND THE GRAY SISTERS

When Perseus reached their dwelling the door was wide-open, and so he walked in. He was overjoyed to find the three sisters all taking a nap, with their one eye and one tooth lying beside them; and he quickly seized both these treasures. That done, he awakened the sisters and inquired of them the way to the home of the Hesperides. At first they refused to tell him, but when they found that he had their eye and tooth, they quickly told him how to go. He then gave them back the eye and the tooth.

PERSEUS AND THE HESPERIDES

It did not take him long to reach the home of the Hesperides. It was an island in the Western Ocean. The nymphs had been told by Minerva that he was coming. So when he arrived they gave him welcome and agreed to lend him their magic treasures.

"The distance across the sea to the home of the Gorgons is great," said one of the nymphs to Perseus. "Take therefore these winged sandals of gold. With them you can fly through the air like an eagle."

"The Gorgon's head," said another of the nymphs, "must be kept in this magic wallet, lest you look upon the terrible face and be turned to stone."

"To get near the Gorgons," added the third, "you must wear this cap of darkness, so that you may see without being seen."

The hero then slung the wallet over his shoulder, put the sandals upon his feet, and the cap upon his head, and vanished. As swift as lightning, he crossed the dark waters and reached the home of the Gorgons. They were all asleep. Without looking at them Perseus held up the shield of Minerva and saw reflected upon it the frowning face of Medusa. With one blow from the sword of Mercury he struck off her head, and without looking at it placed it within his wallet. Then he hurried away from the weird place.

The other Gorgons awoke at once and followed him in furious haste; but as he wore his cap of darkness they could not see him, and with his sandal wings he flew so fast that he was soon too far for them to follow.

PART Ii

AS he was flying along the coast of Africa he heard the sound of weeping. He looked down and saw a beautiful girl chained to a rock at the water's edge. Hastening to her, he took off his cap of darkness that she might see him and exclaimed, "Fair maiden, why are you chained to this rock?"

"Alas!" she said, "I have been offered as a sacrifice to Neptune. You cannot save me, however much you want to."

Her words made Perseus the more determined to help her. "Why is Neptune angry?" he asked. "And who has dared to treat you so cruelly?"

"I am Andromeda, daughter of Cepheus and Cassiopeia, king and queen of this land," replied the maiden. "My mother boasted that I was more beautiful than any nymph in Neptune's palace. Her pride enraged Neptune so that he raised great storms and sent a terrible monster to devour our people. The priests said that if I were offered to him the rest of the people would be spared."

Then with the sword of light Perseus cut the chain which bound Andromeda to the rock. At this moment the monster, huge and ugly, came plowing through the water. Perseus could not be seen because he had put on his cap of darkness, and before the creature could harm the maiden its head was cut off by the sword of light.

On his swift-winged sandals Perseus, with Andromeda in his arms, now flew to the palace of Cepheus and Cassiopeia.

PERSEUS SLAYS
THE GORGON

There had been many glad weddings before that of Perseus and Andromeda, but none was ever more joyful. For he was admired as a wonderful hero, and everyone loved the girl who had been willing to give her life to save her people.

After the wedding Perseus went back to Seriphos, taking Andromeda with him. When

PERSEUS RESCUES ANDROMEDA

he reached the island Polydectes was in his palace feasting, and Perseus hastened at once to the banquet hall and said to the king:

"See! I have brought that which you desired."

With these words he held up the head of the Gorgon. The king and his courtiers gave one look and were instantly turned to stone.

The Gorgon's head had now done its work; so Perseus carried it to a temple of Minerva and there offered it to the goddess. Ever after she wore it upon her shield, and its snaky ringlets and frowning face are to be seen upon her statues. The sword of light was given back to

Mercury, who also returned the winged sandals, the magic wallet and the cap of darkness to the Hesperides.

PART III

YOU will remember that Argos was the birthplace of Perseus, and to that city he now returned, taking Andromeda with him. His grandfather, who was still king of Argos, remembered the oracle that he should die by the hand of Danaë's son and was much alarmed, but Perseus quieted the fears of the king and the two became very good friends. While playing quoits one day, however, Perseus accidentally hit his grandfather with a quoit. The wound caused the old king's death. And thus, as the Greeks used to say, "What had been fated came to pass."

Perseus was overwhelmed with sorrow. He could not bear to live any longer at Argos and therefore gave his kingdom to a kinsman of his, in exchange for the kingdom of Tiryns.

At Tiryns he ruled long and wisely. The gods gave him and Andromeda a glorious place among the stars after their death. With Cepheus and Cassiopeia they can still be seen in the skies not far from where the Great Bear shines.

Chapter 5

Hercules and His Labors

PART I

GREATEST of all the heroes of Greece was Herakles, or Hercules, who was born in Thebes, the city of Cadmus. His mother was one of the descendants of Perseus and his father was Jupiter. Juno, the queen of the gods, hated Hercules. When he was only a baby in the cradle she sent two large serpents to devour him. He grasped the throat of each serpent with his tiny fingers and choked both to death.

When he had grown to manhood he was forced by the will of the gods to become the slave of a hardhearted cousin of his named Eurystheus, who was king of Mycenæ.

Eurystheus set twelve tasks for Hercules. The first was to kill the Nemean lion. This was a ferocious animal that lived in the forest of Nemea and ate a child or a grown person every two or three days. Its skin was so tough that nothing could pierce it, but Hercules drove the lion before him into a cave and, following boldly, grasped the beast about the neck and choked it to death. That done, he stripped off its skin, which he ever after wore as a cloak.

HERCULES AND THE SERPENTS

When the Nemean lion had been killed Eurystheus said to Hercules, "You must now kill the hydra that lives in the marsh of Lerna. "

This hydra was a nine-headed water serpent whose very breath was poisonous. It was hard to kill the creature because as soon as one head was cut off two others at once sprang up in its place. This task might have proved too much for Hercules if a friend had not prevented new heads from growing by burning each neck with a firebrand the instant that Hercules cut off the head.

The third of Hercules' tasks was to bring to Eurystheus the stag with golden horns that was sacred to Diana. It lived in southern Greece in the woods of Arcadia. It had brazen feet and could run so fast that Hercules had to chase it for a whole year before he caught it.

"Now," said Eurystheus, "you must kill the boar that roams on the slopes of Mount Erymanthus." This creature laid waste the farmers' fields of barley and wheat at the foot of the mountain. Hercules captured the brute in a net and killed it.

The next command of Eurystheus to Hercules was, "Clean the Augean stables."

The Augean stables belonged to Augeas, one of the kings of Greece. As three thousand oxen were kept in them, and as they had not been cleaned for thirty years, they were filthy. Hercules cleaned them in one day. He dug a great ditch as far as the stables and turned into it the waters of two swift rivers.

PART II

AS soon as this was done Eurystheus said, "you must now kill the birds of Lake Stymphalus." Instead of wings of feathers these birds had wings of arrows which darted out and shot any one who passed by. Their claws and beaks were of brass, and they fed on human flesh. Hercules killed them with poisoned arrows.

Still Eurystheus hoped to find some task that might prove too much for the hero, so he said, "Bring me the bull of Crete."

This bull was a terrible monster that had been sent by Neptune to ravage Crete, an island not far from Greece. Hercules set out for Crete at once, conquered the bull, rode on his back across the sea from Crete to Greece, then swung the great animal to his own shoulders and carried him to Eurystheus.

Eurystheus now said to his wonderful slave, "Tame the man-eating horses of Diomedes, king of Thrace." He fully expected that this task would be fatal to Hercules. But the hero went to the palace of Diomedes and soon discovered a way to tame the savage steeds. He killed Diomedes and threw his flesh to them, when lo! the man-eating beasts became like other horses and gladly ate oats and grass.

Eurystheus immediately set a ninth task.

"My daughter," said he, "wants the girdle of the queen of the Amazons. Get it for her."

The Amazons were a nation living upon the shores of the Black Sea. It was the custom for the women to go to battle. Bravest of them all was Queen Hippolyte, whom Mars had rewarded for her courage by giving her a beautiful girdle. All Greece had heard of this girdle, and it was no wonder that the daughter of Eurystheus wished to have it.

When Hercules reached the country of the Amazons and made known his errand he found that the queen was as generous as she was brave. She said that she would send her girdle as a present to the daughter of Eurystheus. So it looked as though Hercules was to have no trouble at all with this task. Juno, however, tried to prevent his success. She made herself look like one of the Amazons and went among them and persuaded them that Hercules wished to carry away their queen. A great quarrel then arose between the hero and the Amazons, which ended in a battle. Brave Hippolyte was killed, and Hercules then took the girdle and carried it to Eurystheus.

PART III

"BRING me the oxen of Geryon," Eurystheus now commanded.

Geryon was a monster with three bodies. He lived on an island in the Western Ocean, as the Greeks called the Atlantic Ocean. In the fields of this island grazed Geryon's herd of red oxen guarded by a two-headed dog. At first Hercules did not see how he could reach the island. But the sun-god, Apollo, came to his aid and said to him, "I will lend you the golden bowl in which I sail every night from the land of the Western Sea to the land of the rising sun."

So in the sun's golden bowl Hercules reached the island safely. He slew the two-headed dog, then got the whole herd of oxen into the golden bowl and sailed back.

For the tenth time Eurystheus was amazed. He now commanded Hercules, "Get me some of the apples of the Hesperides."

At the wedding of Jupiter and Juno, the grandest that ever took place on Olympus, Ceres, the great earth-mother, had given to Juno some branches loaded with golden apples. These branches were afterwards planted and grew into trees upon islands in the Western Ocean, far away from Greece. The trees and their fruit were in charge of the nymphs called Hesperides, who had a terrible dragon to aid them. When Hercules was told to get some of the apples of the Hesperides he was puzzled. At last he went to Atlas, who was the father of the Hesperides, and begged his help. Atlas lived in Africa, opposite Spain. His duty was to hold up the sky, with all it contains, the sun, moon and stars.

"I will get you some of the apples," said Atlas in answer to Hercules, "if you will hold up the sky for me while I am getting them."

The bargain was made. Hercules held up the sky while Atlas went and secured three of the golden apples. Then the giant took the sky again on his shoulders, and Hercules carried the apples to Eurystheus.

The Fates allowed Eurystheus to send Hercules upon only one more of his dangerous errands.

"Go to the gates of the underworld," said Eurystheus, "and bring Cerberus here."

Hercules now, if ever, had need of aid from the gods. They did not fail him. Mercury, the god who guided the souls of the dead to the unseen world, and Minerva, the goddess of wisdom, both went with him to the kingdom of Pluto.

Pluto said that if Hercules could overpower Cerberus without using any weapon he might take the great watchdog to the world of light. Hercules wrestled with the monster, overcame him, and dragged him to the palace of Eurystheus.

This ended the power of Eurystheus over the hero.

THE DAUGHTERS OF ATLAS

HERCULES AS THE SLAVE OF OMPHALE

PART IV

HERCULES had a friend named Admetus, a king in Thessaly, who was about to die. The Fates had promised that his life should be spared if his father, mother or wife would die for him. When both father and mother refused, Alcestis, his wife, gave her life for him. Admetus was crazed with grief at losing her, and so Hercules went to Pluto's kingdom, seized Alcestis, and brought her to her husband.

Once Hercules became insane and killed a friend whom he greatly loved. The gods punished him for this with a serious sickness. He asked Apollo to cure him, but the god refused, and Hercules tried to carry away the tripod on which the priestess of Delphi sat when the god spoke to her. For this he was deprived of his great strength and given as a slave to Omphale, Queen of Lydia. She took the Nemean lion's skin from him and dressed him as a woman. Then she made him kneel at her feet and spin thread and do a woman's work for three years. After he was again free he did many brave deeds.

Once when journeying with his wife Deianira he reached a river. There was neither bridge nor ferry. Nessus, the centaur, half-man, half-horse, who owned that part of the river, undertook to carry Deianira across while Hercules waded. When Nessus reached the middle of the river he tried to run away with Deianira, but Hercules shot him with one of his poisoned arrows. Nessus, while dying, told Deianira to save some of his blood and use it as a charm to make Hercules love her more.

NESSUS CARRYING OFF DEIANIRA

PART IV

SOME years after this, Deianira became very jealous, and the foolish woman sprinkled some drops of the centaur's poisoned blood upon a robe that Hercules had to wear at a sacrifice. When Hercules put on the robe the poison burned like fire. He tried to pull off the garment, but it clung to him, and as he pulled it his flesh was torn.

Seeing now that his end was near, he went to the top of a mountain. There he pulled up some trees by the roots and heaped them together to make his funeral pyre. With his club for a pillow and his lion's skin for a cover, he lay upon the pyre and soon he ceased to breathe. A friend kindled the pyre, and the hero's body was burned to ashes. Then a cloud, gleaming as though on fire, descended through the air, and amid the pealing of thunder the mighty spirit was born to the skies.

There Jupiter made him one of the gods and gave him the beautiful goddess Hebe for a wife.

Chapter 6

Jason and the Golden Fleece

PART I

IN a city of Greece named Iolcus a good man called Æson was king. His younger brother, Pelias, seized the throne. But Pelias did not enjoy much happiness in his stolen kingdom. He had no fear of Æson, who was a weak man. But he was very much afraid that Æson's son Jason, then only a boy, might some day take the kingdom from him.

So he tried to kill Jason, but the child was taken away by night and Pelias never found him. It was said that he was dead. Twenty years passed, and though Jason was never seen in Iolcus Pelias was still afraid that he was alive. Finally, to settle the matter, he consulted the oracle of Apollo.

He received the answer, "Beware of the man who wears but one sandal." After that Pelias ordered the watchman at the city gate to take notice of the feet of every stranger who entered the city.

JASON

Jason had been all these years in charge of Chiron, the centaur, who was the most famous teacher in Greece. Jason had heard of the wicked- ness of his uncle, and now that he was a man he determined to regain his father's kingdom.

So one day he set out for Iolcus. On the way he came to a wide stream over which there was no bridge. At the same time a feeble old woman came up and wished to cross. The stream was swollen, and it looked as if she would be swept away by the current and drowned if she tried to wade across. So Jason took her in his arms and carried her over.

That old woman was really Juno, the queen of the gods. She had come down from Olympus to take a journey on earth without telling any one who she was, because she wished to find out if there was any real kindness among men. She never forgot Jason's courtesy; and to her help he owed his success in his career.

In crossing the stream he lost one of his sandals, and so he reached Iolcus with one foot bare. He cared very little about this; but when word was brought to Pelias that a man wearing one sandal had entered the city, the king was greatly alarmed.

"Either I must kill that man," Pelias said to himself, "or he will kill me." He therefore sent a messenger to invite the stranger to the palace, and Jason soon stood before him.

"What would you do," asked Pelias, "if you had in your power the man who was fated to kill you?"

"I should tell him," answered Jason, "to go to Colchis and bring me 'the golden fleece.'
"

"Then you shall go," cried Pelias, "You have come to take my kingdom from me; but not till you bring me that fleece will I yield you my crown."

The story of the golden fleece is very interesting.

Many years before one of the Grecian kings, who had a son named Phrixus, was told by an oracle that Jupiter wished him to offer up his son as a sacrifice. The poor father prepared to make the offering. As the young man was standing before the altar and his father was just about to slay him, a ram with shining fleece of gold came down from the sky and stood beside them. Phrixus jumped to the back of the ram. His sister, Helle, who was standing with him at the altar, jumped on behind her brother, and the ram immediately ran off with the two. He went so fast that people who saw him thought he had wings. When he came to the strait which separates Europe from Asia he plunged into the waves. Poor Helle soon fell off and was drowned; and ever after that the strait was called by the Greeks the Hellespont, a word that means the Sea of Helle. It is the strait that is named the Dardanelles' on our maps.

The ram carried Phrixus safely across the strait, and went on until he reached the palace of Æetes the king of a country called Colchis, which lay on the shores of the Euxine, or Black Sea.

GREEK SANDALS

Phrixus felt very thankful for having made such a wonderful journey in safety, so he offered the ram as a sacrifice to Jupiter and nailed the fleece to a tree that was sacred to Mars.

This fleece became one of the wonders of the world; and lest it should be stolen a dragon was set to watch it. Many persons tried to get possession of it, but most, if not all of them, lost their lives in the attempt.

Jason knew all this, but he said at once that he would get the fleece. Before setting out on the journey, however, he went to a place called Dodona to ask the advice of Jupiter; for at Dodona there was a wonderful talking oak which told men the advice and commands of Jupiter. As soon as Jason came near the oak the leaves began to rustle, and a voice from within the tree said:

"Build a fifty-oared ship. Take as companions the greatest heroes of Greece. Cut a branch from the talking oak and make it a part of the prow of the vessel."

All these commands Jason obeyed. The ship was built and a piece of the talking oak was used in making her prow. Jason invited forty-nine of the bravest men of Greece to go on the expedition. He named his ship the Argo, and he and his companions are known as the Argonauts, or sailors on the Argo. One of them was Orpheus, the greatest musician that ever played or sang in Greece. It was said of him that the trees of a forest once danced in wild delight at his music.

This wonderful musician was of very great use on the Argo. The ship was the largest that had ever been built in Greece and it was found too heavy to launch. The strength of all the fifty heroes did not move it an inch. Jason did not know what to do. So he consulted the talking prow, which told him that everybody must get on board and that Orpheus must then play his lyre and sing. No sooner was the music heard than the great ship glided easily into the water, and the famous voyage began.

Another companion of Jason was Hercules, about whose wonderful labors you have already been told. Then there were Castor and Pollux, twin brothers, who did such wonders that after their death the gods took them to heaven, where they still shine as stars in the constellation called the "Twins."

Still another of the Argonauts was a hero named Lynceus, which means the lynx-eyed. He was kept on watch all through the Argo's voyage, because he could see a whole day's trip ahead.

PART II

AFTER many adventures the Argonauts at last crossed the Black Sea and reached the shores of Colchis. Æetes received them in a kind manner; but he was not at all pleased when he learned their errand, because there was nothing in his kingdom which he prized so much as the golden fleece.

However, when Jason explained the matter, Æetes said, "Very will, you may try to get the fleece if you choose to run the risk. But first you must yoke my pair of brazen-footed, fire-breathing bulls and with them plow a field near the grove where the golden fleece hangs. Then you must sow the field with some of the teeth of the dragon that Cadmus killed. And finally, you must fight with the dragon that guards the fleece."

Æetes felt sure that Jason would lose his life in trying to do all this; for many brave men had been burned to death in the streams of fire that the bulls breathed out from their nostrils.

King Æetes had a daughter named Medea. She was famed for her beauty and her skill as an enchantress. Fortunately, she fell in love with Jason and now came to his aid.

"Take this ointment," said Medea, "and rub it all over your body. Then the flaming breath of the bulls cannot harm you. At midnight I will go with you to the pasture where the creatures feed."

That night Jason went with Medea and found the bulls in the pasture. The magic ointment saved him from being burned by their fiery breath. He seized and yoked them without any trouble, and very soon the field was plowed and harrowed. Jason sowed the teeth of the dragon and then stood waiting to see what would happen.

Soon points of light glistened here and there in the soil. They were the tops of helmets coming up out of the ground and touched by the rays of the rising sun. In no great while where each point of light had appeared stood a full-armed warrior.

"Throw a stone into the midst of the host!" commanded Medea; and Jason obeyed.

The stone struck one warrior, glanced off to another, and then to a third. The new-born heroes, not knowing whence the stone had come, became wild with rage, and hacked and battered one another with swords and clubs. At last only one was left and he was fatally wounded.

Then Jason went back to the palace and told Æetes what he had done, and said that he was ready to fight the dragon that guarded the golden fleece.

MEDEA MIXING
AN ENCHANTED POTION

At midnight he went with Medea to the grove in which the fleece hung. The dragon rushed with wide-open jaws to devour him, but Medea threw an enchanted potion into the monster's mouth, and he sank to the ground in a death-like sleep.

"Make haste!" cried Medea. "Take down the fleece." In a twinkling Jason had done so. "And now," she added, "we must start at once for Greece; for my father will never let you carry the fleece from Colchis."

Taking Medea with him, Jason made all haste to the Argo. When he reached the shore where the ship lay, his companions welcomed him heartily, and they were filled with delight when they saw the golden fleece. All hurried on board the Argo, the sails were hoisted, and the ship began her homeward voyage.

To get back to Greece the Argonauts had to sail past the Isle of the Sirens. The sirens were maidens with beautiful faces but cruel hearts. They sat upon dangerous rocks on the shore of their island and sang songs of enchanting sweetness. Sailors who heard them would steer nearer and nearer, till their vessels were wrecked on the jagged rocks. The Argonauts escaped this peril through the help of Orpheus. He played his lyre and sang more sweetly than even the Sirens, and listening to him, Jason and his companions steered their vessel beyond the dangerous rocks.

As soon as Jason reached Iolcus again he showed the golden fleece to Pelias, and then hung it up as a thank-offering in the temple of one of the gods. What became of it afterward nobody knows.

While Jason was getting the golden fleece Pelias murdered Æson. In revenge for this Medea made a plot by which Pelias was killed by his own daughters. Then the son of Pelias drove both Jason and Medea from Iolcus.

Chapter 7

Theseus

PART I

ONE of the most violent quarrels that ever disturbed the life of the gods was between Neptune and Minerva.

Cecrops, one of the wisest of the Greeks, was founding a city near the finest harbor in Greece. Neptune wished to be the chief god of the city, and Minerva also desired the honor.

Neptune said that as the city was going to be a great seaport, busy with vessels sailing in and sailing out, it was only right that he, the god of the ocean should be its guardian.

Minerva foresaw that in days to come the men of the city would care much less about commerce than about art and learning. She therefore thought that she, the goddess of wisdom, should be its guardian.

The other gods became very weary of the quarrel, and to bring it to an end Jupiter ordered that the one who should offer the more useful gift to the city should become its chief god.

Neptune then struck with his trident a rock within the city's bounds, and up sprang a war horse ready for battle. Minerva touched the earth, and an olive tree rose on the spot.

Now groves of olive trees, Jupiter knew well, would be far more useful to the people than the finest of war horses. He therefore decided in favor of Minerva. The city became the most famous place in all the world for learning and art, and from Athene, the Greek name of the goddess, it was called Athens.

THE GIFTS OF MINERVA
AND NEPTUNE

PART II

The most noted of the early kings of Athens was Theseus, the son of Ægeus, who was himself a king of Athens. Theseus was born far away from Athens and was brought up by his mother, Æthra, at the home of her father.

Before parting with Æthra at her father's home, Ægeus placed a sword and a pair of sandals under a heavy stone and said to her:

"When the child is able to lift that stone, let him take the sandals and sword and come to me."

Years went by, and when Theseus had grown up, his mother led him one day to the stone and said to him:

"If you are a man, lift that stone."

Theseus lifted it with ease and saw a pair of sandals and a sword.

His mother told him that the sandals and the sword had been placed under the stone by his father, Ægeus, who was king of Athens. "Put them on and seek him in Athens," she said.

He fastened the sword to his girdle and buckled the sandals on his feet. Then he kissed his mother and set out for Athens.

He did not go far without an adventure. A robber called the Club-bearer attacked him. A struggle followed, in which the Club-bearer was killed. Then Theseus took the robber's club and ever after that carried it himself.

A little farther on he met a robber called Sinis, who was known as the Pine-bender. It was the Pine-bender's sport to pull down pine trees, tie travelers to their tops, and let the trees spring back. His victims dangled from the tree-tops until they perished from pain and hunger. When Theseus came along he bent a pine, fastened the Pine-bender to it, let the tree spring back, and left the robber to suffer the torture that he had inflicted on so many others.

Journeying still farther, the hero reached the dwelling of Procrustes, the Stretcher. Procrustes had a bed which he made all travelers fit. If a man's legs were too long, Procrustes cut them to the right length. If they were too short, he stretched them until they were long enough. Theseus forced Procrustes to lie upon the bed himself and chopped the Stretcher's legs to the right length.

In this manner, fighting often and bravely, Theseus made his way to Athens. When he reached the city and showed his sword to Ægeus, the king knew that the young man must be his son. He was filled with joy and declared Theseus his heir.

PART III

Every year the city of Athens had to send seven young men and seven maidens to Minos, the king of Crete, to be devoured by a terrible creature, called the Minotaur. It was kept in a place known as the Labyrinth. The Labyrinth was full of winding paths, so puzzling that a person, once in, could not find his way out.

The day that the youths and maidens were to sail to Crete was at hand, and Athens was filled with sorrow. Theseus made up his mind that never again should the city have cause for such grief. He determined to kill the Minotaur.

"Father," he said to Ægeus, "let me go to Crete as one of the victims."

"No, no, my son!" cried Ægeus, "I could not bear to lose you."

"Ah, but you will not lose me," answered Theseus. "Not only shall I return, but I will bring back in safety all who go with me."

Ægeus at last gave consent and Theseus

VICTIMS OF THE MINOTAUR AT THE DOOR OF THE LABYRINTH

went as one of the fourteen victims.

The ship's sail was black, an emblem of mourning. As Theseus bade farewell to his father, he said, "I am taking a white sail with me to hoist when we come back. If the black sail should still be set when the ship comes home you will know that I have failed. But I shall not fail."

When the black-sailed vessel reached the shores of Crete there was a great crowd gathered to see the victims. Among the watchers was Ariadne, the lovely daughter of the king of Crete. She was full of pity for those who were to be devoured. When she was told that Theseus had determined to fight the Minotaur, she made up her mind to help him. She could see that he was very strong and she felt sure that he could kill the monster. But she feared that he would starve to death in the Labyrinth because he would not be able to find his way out. So when Theseus went into the Labyrinth she gave him the end of a ball of thread and said:

"I will stand here at the entrance and let the ball unwind as you go in. When you have killed the Minotaur follow the thread back to me."

THE MINOTAUR

So Theseus took hold of the thread and went boldly into the Labyrinth. When he reached the center of it the monster came to attack him. Its weapons were stones. Stone

28

after stone was flung by the monster but each was warded off by Theseus, just as a skilful batter wards off a swift ball. At length Theseus was close enough to strike the Minotaur with his sword and the creature fell dead.

Guided by the thread, Theseus quickly made his way back to the entrance of the Labyrinth. There he was joyfully received by Ariadne and the youths and maidens whom he had saved from death.

Theseus and Ariadne had fallen in love with each other, and when the tribute ship set sail for Greece Ariadne was one of the passengers.

On the homeward voyage the ship touched at the island of Naxos. There Theseus had a strange dream. In it he was told by Minerva to leave Ariadne on the island because the Fates intended her to be the wife of one of the gods.

ARIADNE

Accordingly, on the island of Naxos he left her, and sailed away to Greece. She afterward did become the bride of one of the gods, who gave her a golden crown, which after her death was changed to a crown of stars that is yet to be seen in the sky on any bright night.

On the voyage from the island of Naxos to Athens, Theseus was thinking so much of Ariadne that he quite forgot to change the black sail for the white one, as he had promised his father to do. This was a most unfortunate oversight, for it brought death to Ægeus and sorrow to Theseus.

Day after day, while Theseus was away, Ægeus had sat on a cliff which overlooked the sea, hoping to catch sight of the white sail. When at last the ship appeared with its black sail still spread, the poor king supposed of course that his son had been devoured by the Minotaur. He threw up his hands in grief, and falling from the cliff into the sea, was drowned. From that day to this the sea has been called the Ægean, or the sea of Ægeus.

When the ship reached the harbor of Athens, Theseus learned of his father's death, and bitterly did he mourn that he had forgotten to hoist the white sail.

He at once became king; and no king ever did more for Athens than he. Yet in spite of his love and labor for the city, the Athenians were not grateful. After a while he went on a journey. He remained away for so long that they chose a new king. When at last he came back and found that the people whom he had loved so well had forgotten him, he left the city and soon died.

The Athenians in later days repented that they had been so ungrateful. They brought his bones to Athens and buried them with great solemnity. Festivals were held in his honor, and he was ranked almost with Minerva herself as a guardian of the beautiful city.

The story is told that centuries after his death he left the spirit-world and helped the Athenians to gain the victory in the greatest battle they ever fought, the battle of Marathon, of which you will read farther on in this book.

Chapter 8

Agamemnon

THE early kings of Mycenæ were descendants of Jupiter. One of these, named Agamemnon, was the most powerful king in Greece in his day, and hence he was called the "King of Men." During his reign occurred the famous Trojan War, which is supposed to have taken place about years before Christ. All the most famous heroes in Greece took part in it. The story of the events that brought it on is full of interest.

A wonderful wedding took place in Greece. Peleus, the brave king of Thessaly, married the beautiful sea-nymph, Thetis. The wedding feast was held on Mount Pelion near the home of the gods, and to show their love for Thetis all the gods came down from Olympus. Apollo shot sunbeams through the quivering oak leaves and the floor of the forest was dappled with golden light. Nymphs had hung garlands of snow-white roses from tree to tree. Wild vines were covered with blossoms and the air was filled with their fragrance.

But while the Muses were singing their sweetest songs, a golden apple suddenly fell among the gods and goddesses. It had been thrown by the goddess of discord, who was angry because she had not been asked to the wedding.

Mercury, who of course was among the guests, picked up the apple and read to the wedding party the words written upon it, "Let the most beautiful have me."

Juno, Minerva, and Venus each claimed that the apple was hers, and the quarrel of the goddesses ended only when Jupiter said to them:

"Go with Mercury over the sea to Mount Ida, and let Paris, the shepherd, decide the matter."

At once the goddesses, led by Mercury, sped through the air to Mount Ida to find Paris.

Paris was a son of Priam, the king of a rich and powerful city called Troy, which was opposite Greece on the shore of the Ægean Sea. His mother dreamed that he would one day set Troy on fire, and so, as soon as he was born, King Priam ordered one of his shepherds to carry the infant to snow- capped Mount Ida, near Troy, and there leave it to die of cold and hunger.

HEROES OF THE TROJAN WAR

Five days after leaving the child, the shepherd found it still alive. This made him think that the gods did not wish it to die; so he carried it home to his wife, who brought it up as her own child.

Paris thought himself only a shepherd's boy and tended King Priam's herds while they grazed on the slopes of Mount Ida.

On the date of the wedding upon Mount Pelion, as he sat watching the flock, Mercury and his three companions suddenly appeared before him. The goddesses were all so lovely that when they asked Paris to say which was the most beautiful he was greatly perplexed. Each tried to persuade him to decide in her favor. Juno promised to make him the greatest of kings; Minerva said that she would make him the wisest of men; and Venus declared that she would give him the most beautiful woman in the world as his wife. He awarded the apple to Venus, but by doing so he greatly offended Minerva and Juno.

PARIS

Not long after this Paris went to Troy and took part in some games that were held at the court of Priam. These games were wrestling, boxing and running races; and the unknown shepherd carried off many prizes. It was soon found out who he really was and Priam heartily welcomed him home.

PARIS GIVES THE APPLE TO VENUS

Meantime, Venus had not forgotten her promise. She advised Paris to sail to Greece, where he would find the most beautiful woman in the world. This was Helen, the wife of Menelaus, king of Sparta.

Paris went to Sparta and with the help of Venus won the heart of Helen and took her away with him to Troy.

When Menelaus found that his wife had been stolen he sent a message to the kings of all the states of Greece and asked them to help him to regain Helen and punish Paris. Now thirty or more of the kings had wished to marry Helen before she had chosen a husband, and all had sworn to aid the one chosen if any one should ever try to take her away from her husband. So as soon as they received the message of Menelaus, in accord with their oath these kings began to make ready for war against the Trojans.

Meanwhile Agamemnon, who was a brother of Menelaus, was already busily preparing for war. His woodsmen were cutting yew trees from which to make bows and gathering reeds for arrows. His smiths were making swords and spear-heads and javelins. In his shipyards hundreds of men were building ships. The roads were alive with countrymen bringing in loads of wheat, barley, bacon, and olives to store in the vessels.

HELEN OF TROY

At last one hundred black ships were ready and Agamemnon set sail. A place named Aulis had been selected where the Greeks were to meet. Twelve hundred ships assembled there, and Agamemnon was chosen commander-in-chief.

Just as the ships were about to start for Troy a terrible storm came up. Agamemnon felt sure that one of the gods must be angry with the Greeks and so he consulted a wonderful soothsayer named Calchas.

"Diana is angry, great King," said Calchas, "but not with the Greeks. Thou only hast offended her. Thou hast slain a deer in the forest and boasted that thou hast greater skill in the chase than Diana herself. Never, O King," he added, "can the storm be lulled until thou hast offered thy daughter Iphigenia as a sacrifice on the altar of Diana."

Agamemnon was heart-broken, but he felt that the will of Diana must be done. So he sent a messenger to the mother of Iphigenia to say that Achilles, a Greek prince, wished to marry the girl and that she must come to Aulis at once. This was only a device to get Iphigenia to Aulis.

However, when she reached Aulis and heard the truth from her father, the girl behaved nobly. "My father," she said, "if my death will help the Greeks, I am ready to die."

THE SACRIFICE OF IPHIGENIA

Her words sent a thrill through all the host and ninety thousand brave men sorrowed. Achilles and Ajax, sternest of warriors, wept, and Agamemnon was wild with grief.

While the girl was lying upon the altar and the priestess of Diana was standing near, the goddess, watching from Olympus, was moved to pity; and, just as the father had lifted his swords to slay the girl, a cloud as bright as shining snow appeared above him. Diana stepped from the cloud, lifted the girl from the altar, and carried her through the air to one of her temples, where she made her a priestess. On the altar lay a white fawn which was sacrificed instead of Iphigenia.

And now the fairest winds blew, the sails of the Grecian ships were set, the fleet sailed swiftly to Troy, and the siege of that city began.

Chapter 9

Achilles: Bravest of Greeks

BRAVEST of all the Greeks who went to fight the Trojans was Achilles. He was the son of Peleus and the beautiful sea-nymph Thetis, at whose marriage feast the goddess of discord had thrown the golden apple among the guests.

Thetis herself could never die, and when Achilles was born she determined to make him also immortal. With the child in her arms she went down to the gloomy kingdom of Hades. You will remember that a dark river called the Styx flowed round the underworld. If a mortal were dipped into the Styx no sword or arrow or other weapon could injure him. Thetis held Achilles by the heel and dipped him into the water. In her haste to get out of the underworld she forgot to dip in the heel by which she had held the child. So in that heel, and only there, Achilles could be wounded.

When Thetis heard that the Greeks were going to fight the Trojans she was greatly distressed, for she knew that if her son went to the war he would certainly lose his life. She dressed him as a girl and took him to Scyros, a far away island of Greece, and left him there in the palace of the king Lycomedes.

Now Calchas had foretold that Troy could never be taken without the help of Achilles. So the Greek princes were determined that he should go with them.

A Grecian chief, called Ulysses the crafty, learned where he was hidden and set out to find him.

One day a peddler appeared at the gate of the palace in Scyros, bringing all sorts of beautiful things for sale. The princesses were wild with delight as the peddler showed one thing after another. Suddenly the blast of a war trumpet rang through the air. Away ran all the girls save one. That one seized a shield and a spear which were among the peddler's wares and stood instantly ready for battle.

ACHILLES AT THE COURT
OF LYCOMEDES

Then the peddler, who was Ulysses, knew that he had found Achilles. So he told the young man that all the princes of the Greeks were preparing for war against Troy. Achilles was eager to go with them, and so in spite of all that

TROJANS TRYING TO BURN
THE GREEK SHIPS

Thetis had done, her son sailed to Troy with the other Greek princes. For nine years he was the champion of the Greeks.

In the tenth year of the war a great misfortune befell the Greeks. They had taken captive two beautiful maidens, one of whom had been given as a slave to Achilles, the other to Agamemnon. Now it happened that Agamemnon's slave was the daughter of Chryses, a priest of the sun-god Apollo.

The loss of his daughter was a great grief to Chryses, and he prayed to Apollo for vengeance. In answer Apollo drew his silver bow and shot arrows which brought a terrible pestilence into the camp of the Greeks. The tents were soon filled with the dead and the dying.

The soothsayer, Calchas, told the Greeks why Apollo had punished them, and the girl was sent back to her father. The god was satisfied, and his arrows stopped bringing the plague to the Greeks.

But Agamemnon now took the other maiden from Achilles, and this made the son of Thetis so angry that he declared he would help the Greeks no more. For days and days he stayed in his tent, or sat by the seashore and told his wrongs to his mother.

Then the Trojans, learning that Achilles was not fighting, grew bold and at last came out through the gates of their city and drove the Greeks from the field. Hector, a son of Priam, followed them to their ships. Some of the Trojans took lighted torches and tried to burn the Greek fleet. One ship caught fire.

Just then, however, there rushed to the shore a warrior who looked so like Achilles that the Trojans fled from the ships to the gates of their city. The unknown warrior was not Achilles but Patroclus, his devoted friend, who had put on Achilles' armor. The Trojans had mistaken him for the great hero. Even Hector fled before him. But Apollo, who fought on the side of the Trojans, at last shot forth from his silver bow an arrow which struck Patroclus,

NEPTUNE RISES FROM THE SEA
TO HELP THE GREEKS

and he fell to the earth. Hector then slew him and carried off the armor of Achilles as his prize.

When Achilles learned that his friend had been slain he forgot his wrongs and rushed from his tent, shouting the war-cry of the Greeks. He had neither shield nor spear. Yet the Trojans fled at the sound of his voice; and the ships and tents of the Greeks were saved.

The body of Patroclus was then carried into the tent of Achilles, and the hero wept for his friend.

As he sat mourning his mother Thetis rose from her home in the sea and came to comfort him. She then went to Vulcan the great blacksmith, who, you remember, made all things of iron and bronze for the gods, and said:

"Good Vulcan, make for my son such a suit of armor as never mortal has worn."

Soon the forges of Ætna were glowing; the Cyclops' anvils were ringing, and a suit of armor fit for a god was made.

In this armor Achilles made terrible havoc among the Trojans. He scattered them as a wolf might scatter a flock of sheep. He killed Hector at last, tied the body to his chariot, and dragged it three times round the tomb of Patroclus.

Paris avenged the death of Hector by wounding Achilles in the heel. From the wound the great hero died.

THETIS WITH THE
ARMOR OF ACHILLES

ACHILLES WITH HECTOR'S BODY

Hundreds of Trojans had been killed by the Greeks; but the walls of Troy still stood and not one Grecian warrior had entered the gates.

Troy was kept safe in a wonderful way. In the city was an image of Athene, which the Trojans believed had come down from heaven. It was called the Palladium, from Pallas, another name of Athene. So long as the Palladium stood in its place, Troy could never be captured.

At length, crafty Ulysses, with the help of another Greek warrior named Diomedes, got possession of the Palladium. One night the two climbed the walls of Troy, went to the temple where the Palladium was kept, and carried the image away.

THE WOODEN HORSE OF TROY

When they returned to the Grecian camp Ulysses advised the Greeks to build a huge wooden horse. When it was finished it was filled with armed men and left standing before the walls of the city. Then the Grecian army burned their tents and sailed away as if they were going home. But really they only went a short distance and hid behind an island not far from the Trojan coast.

One crafty Greek named Sinon had been left behind. He told the Trojans that the wooden horse would protect their city, just as the Palladium had done. So, very foolishly, they drew the horse within the walls.

When night came Sinon released the armed men from the horse and signalled to the Greek fleet with a flaming torch. In a very short time the ships were all back, and the Greek soldiers again were swarming before the walls of Troy. The city gates were opened by Sinon and his companions, and in poured the Greeks by thousands. They slaughtered the sleeping Trojans, sacked the palace of Priam, and burned the city.

And now, after ten long years of fighting, Mene- laus recovered his beautiful Helen. Then he and the rest of the Greeks set sail for their native land.

THE CAPTIVE ANDROMACHE

Many of the Trojans were carried away into slavery by their Greek conquerors. Andromache, the beautiful wife of Hector, was given to the son of Achilles, who took her home to his palace, a captive.

Chapter 10

The Adventures of Ulysses

PART I

ULYSSES, king of the island of Ithaca, had been very unwilling to go to the Trojan War because there was a prophecy that if he went he would not return for twenty years. So he pretended that he was mad. Yoking an ox and a horse together, he would plow the seashore, and sow the sand with salt.

One of the chiefs suspected that all this was a trick, and to test Ulysses placed the king's infant son Telemachus in front of the plow. Ulysses at once turned the plow to one side and thus showed that he was not mad. He now had no excuse for staying at home and had to go to the war with the other chiefs.

ULYSSES SHOW THAT HIS MADNESS IS A PRETENSE

All through the siege of Troy he was of great value to the Greeks, and after the death of Achilles the splendid armor of that hero was given to Ulysses.

As soon as Troy had fallen he set sail on his homeward voyage. If the winds had been fair he might have reached Ithaca in a month. But the story is that it took him ten years.

He had hardly begun his voyage when his fleet was caught in a storm and his ships were blown to the land of the lotus-eaters. The lotus was a plant that made those who ate it forget their homes and friends forever. Two of Ulysses' sailors went on shore for only a few minutes, and having tasted this curious food became so anxious to stay with the lotus-eaters that they had to be dragged back on board their ship.

After leaving the land of the lotus-eaters the fleet sailed to another shore. The sailors saw the mouth of a cavern and near it large flocks of sheep and goats. Ulysses, with twelve of his men, went to examine the cavern and see if any one lived there. They carried with them a skin full of old wine to give to the king of the island if they should happen to meet him.

They entered the cave and saw pens for sheep and goats. They also found several baskets of cheese. It was plain that somebody lived in the place, so Ulysses decided to wait for the owner and buy some of the cheese from him. Meanwhile he and the sailors helped themselves to what they wanted.

Just as the sun was setting the bleating of sheep and goats was heard, and looking through the mouth of the cave the Greeks saw the owner of the place coming toward them.

He was one of the race of giants called Cyclops, who, you remember, forged lighting and thunder for Jupiter to use in the battles with Cronus. On his back the Cyclops carried a bundle of firewood. Before him went a great flock of sheep and goats. The cave was a shelter for him and his flock.

When the giant had driven the sheep and goats inside he followed them in and closed the entrance with a huge stone. Soon he set about milking the goats. As he milked he muttered that thieves had stolen some of his cheeses. When the milking was over he lighted a fire on the floor of the cave and sat down to a supper of cheese and milk.

The fire lit up the corners of the cave where the Greeks had hidden themselves, and the Cyclops soon saw them.

"Who are you?" he growled. "And what business have you here?"

"Noble Sir, " replied Ulysses, "we are Greeks from the island of Ithaca. With the rest of our nation we have fought against Troy for ten years. At last the city has fallen and now we are sailing homeward. A storm blew us to your island and we landed to look for food. In the name of the blessed gods we ask you to give us something to eat and let us go on our way."

"I care nothing for gods!" roared the Cyclops. "But as for men—let me show you how much I like them!"

With that he seized two of the Greeks and ate them up, devouring even their bones. The other Greeks looked on in terror.

Soon after his supper the Cyclops went to sleep; and Ulysses and his companions would have lost no time in killing him if it had not been for the great stone that blocked the door of the cave. All the Greeks together could not move it, and so they let the Cyclops live because in the morning he would roll the stone away.

Next morning, after devouring two more of the Greeks, he did move the stone; but he put it back as soon as he had driven out his flock, and the Greeks were again shut up. In the evening, after the Cyclops had returned and had supped upon two more Greeks, Ulysses thought of his old wine and asked the giant to taste it. Taste it he did, and then quickly drained three cups.

"What is your name?" asked the Cyclops.

"Noman," answered Ulysses.

"Very well, Noman, you shall be the last that I will eat." And with that the giant lay down in a stupor.

Ulysses had sharpened the trunk of an olive tree that the Cyclops used for a walking cane, and he now held the sharp end in the fire until it glowed. Then with the help of four of his men he rammed the red-hot point into the giant's eye.

The monster roared so loudly that he wakened the other giants who lived in caves nearby, and they came running to ask who had hurt their companion.

"Noman!" screamed the Cyclops. "Noman has put out my eye!"

His friends of course understood him to mean that no one had hurt him. They thought that he had had a terrible nightmare from eating roast cheese and so they went back to their caves.

THE CYCLOPS HURLS STONES
AT ULYSSES

Ulysses now hit on a plan to get his friends and himself safely out of the cave. He bound the big, long-fleeced rams together, three abreast, and fastened a Greek under each middle ram so that every man was completely covered with fleece. He himself managed to cling to a ram that was the largest of the herd.

When the flock was passing out of the cave the Cyclops thought that perhaps the Greeks would try to ride out on the backs of the sheep and goats; so he carefully felt the back of each animal as it went through the door. But he did not feel the Greeks and they all got out safely.

Ulysses then untied his comrades and they ran quickly to their ships, driving before them some of the sheep of the Cyclops. When men and sheep were on board the vessels Ulysses cried out:

"Good-by, Cyclops! What think you now of the gods? They sent me to punish you for your cruelty. Noman is not my name. I am Ulysses, Ithaca's king."

At this the Cyclops picked up great rocks and threw them at the ship of Ulysses. The vessel, however, was not struck, and Ulysses and his men sailed on their way.

PART II

THE next land reached was an island on which Æolus, the god of the winds, had his home. Æolus treated Ulysses very kindly. The west wind, which could carry the ships to Ithaca in nine days, the god left free. All the others he tied up in a stout leather bag, which he gave to the hero. Ulysses then bade farewell to Æolus.

For some time everything went well. One day, however, while Ulysses slept his crew untied the wind bag, hoping to find money in it. As soon as the winds were set free they blew the ships back to the island of Æolus, who drove them off because he thought the gods were angry with them.

The fleet next reached an island where there were cannibals of great size and strength. They broke up all the ships except the one that Ulysses himself commanded, and then feasted on the sailors.

Ulysses made his escape on a single ship with those of his men that were left. He soon arrived at another island, on which at some distance from the shore he saw a marble palace in the middle of a grove. He sent twenty-two men under the charge of his trusty captain Eurylochus to ask for food.

When Eurylochus reached the palace he was met by a troop of lions, tigers and wolves, which capered about and fawned upon him and his men as so many playful puppies might do. This put Eurylochus on his guard. He made up his mind at once that the palace was the home of a wizard or a witch. At the palace gate he inquired, "Who dwells here? We are strangers seeking food."

"Welcome!" replied a voice from within. "Welcome to the palace of the sun-god's daughter. The best that is here shall be yours."

The voice was that of an enchantress called Circe. It was her delight to change men into brutes. The lions, tigers and wolves that had met Eurylochus were really men who had once sat at her table and drunk her enchanted wine.

Eurylochus refused to eat, but the men who went with him were a gluttonous set. They ate greedily and drank deeply. When the feast was at its height Circe touched them with her wand and changed them into hogs.

Eurylochus returned to the ship and told what had happened. Ulysses then hastened to Circe's palace. On the way Mercury met him and walked with him some distance. As they passed through a wood the god plucked some flowers of a plant called moly and gave them to Ulysses.

"Smell them," said Mercury, "while Circe is talking to you and especially when you drink her enchanted wine."

CIRCE AND THE COMPANIONS
OF ULYSSES

When he reached the palace the hero was welcomed as his comrades had been. Circe herself put a golden cup full of wine into his hand. Ulysses took the cup and drained it, taking care all the while to smell the moly that Mercury had given him in the wood.

When the cup was empty the enchantress tapped the hero with her wand and said, "Now, turn to a pig and join your grunting companions."

Unchanged, however, Ulysses drew his sword and cried, "Wicked enchantress, you have no power over me. The gods have sent me here to punish you and you shall die."

"I will undo what I have done if you will spare me," she cried.

So Ulysses followed her to the sty, where she touched the swine, one by one, with her magic wand. As each was touched he was changed back to a man. Next the troop of lions, tigers and wolves were touched, and they too were quickly changed back to men.

The other Greeks were then called from the ships and Circe gave them a feast. After this Ulysses remained on her island for a whole year.

When at last he was going to sail the enchantress gave him some good advice. On the homeward way he and his men would have to pass close to the Isle of the Sirens, as the Argonauts had done long before them.

"To sail by the Sirens' Isle safely," said Circe, "let the men fill their ears with wax and lash you to the mast when the ship draws near to the Isle."

Ulysses and his men then left Circe's island. As they drew near to the Sirens' Isle Ulysses made the sailors fill their ears with wax and lash him to the mast. As they rowed past the Sirens sweet music came over the waters.

"Loose me!" Ulysses cried to his sailors. "Loose me. I must go nearer that music!" But the sailors rowed on. They could hear neither him nor the song of the Sirens.

"Slaves!" cried Ulysses, "Loose me!" But the sailors rowed on.

The music grew fainter and fainter. At last it died away, and the vessel was out of danger. Then the men took the wax from their ears and loosed the cords that bound their chief.

PART III

AFTER passing the Sirens' Isle Ulysses had to sail through a dangerous strait, now know as the Strait of Messina. In a rocky cave on one side of it dwelt a monster called Scylla that had six heads and six mouths. Each mouth could take in a whole man at once. Near the other side of the strait was Charybdis, a whirlpool that sucked down all ships that came near it.

Ulysses saw that he could not escape both these dangers, and so to avoid Charybdis he steered close to Scylla. He ordered his men to row as fast as they could past the monster's cave; and the ship fairly spun through the water. But Scylla was also quick. Darting out all her heads at once, she seized six of the crew. While she was devouring them the ship sped past her, and Ulysses with the rest of his men escaped.

The hero now wished to continue his voyage without stopping, but his comrades were so tired that he agreed to land for the night on the coast of Sicily. So they pulled their ship up the sandy shore and soon all were fast asleep.

In the morning a storm was howling about them. It would have been certain shipwreck to put to sea. The storm raged for a whole month, and even crafty Ulysses did not know what to do.

Worst of all, their provisions began to fail. So the sailors made up their minds to kill some of the famous fat cattle belonging to Apollo that were kept upon the island. Ulysses had been warned not to kill the animals and had ordered his men to leave them alone.

One day, however, when he was away his crew killed some of the cattle. They lit a fire and were roasting several nice pieces of beef when suddenly all started back in terror. The pieces of beef lowed as though they were living and the skins of the slaughtered oxen got up and began to switch their tails and toss their horns and gallop up and down the shore.

The moment the tempest lulled the men dragged their ship down the shore and pushed off as fast as they could.

They were not far out at sea when, suddenly, blackness covered the sky and a dreadful squall blew up. The ship went to pieces and all the men were drowned except Ulysses, who was washed up on the shore of a lonely island.

NAUSICAA AND HER MAIDS

The island was the home of the sea-nymph Ca- lypso. She treated the shipwrecked hero most kindly and became so fond of him that she kept him with her seven years, and promised to make him immortal if he would stay with her always.

But Ulysses longed for home. So at last Calypso led him to the other side of her island, and there he saw a forest of stately pine trees. With a keen bronze axe he soon felled twenty trunks; with these he built a raft, and bidding farewell to Calypso he set out on his homeward voyage.

Soon a storm arose. Heavy waves dashed over the raft and broke it to pieces. The hero clung to one log and drifted on it two days and two nights. The wind then lulled, and Ulysses, seeing land near, swam to the shore. Cold and tired, he gathered dry leaves, lay down upon them, and soon fell asleep. He slept all night and all the next morning.

At noon Nausicaa, the daughter of the king of the island, went to the shore with her maidens. Their talking and laughing awakened Ulysses, and the princess, on hearing the tale of his shipwreck, took him home to her father's palace.

Here he was royally welcomed, and the very next day a ship was made ready and he was sent home to Ithaca.

When at dawn the ship reached Ithaca Ulysses was so fast asleep that the crew carried him out of the vessel, wrapped in the rug on which he was sleeping, and laid him upon the sandy shore without wakening him.

PENELOPE

When he awoke he did not know where he was. But the goddess Minerva appeared and told him that he was on his own island of Ithaca, and that Penelope, his wife, loved him as much as ever. Then he climbed the rocky heights of the island and went to the cottage of his swineherd, who invited him in. Without telling the swineherd who he was he stayed at the cottage that night.

Next morning there appeared at the swineherd's home Ulysses's son, Telemachus, who had just come back from a long search for his father. Ulysses made himself known to his son and they talked over all that had happened while Ulysses had been so far away.

More than a hundred men from Ithaca and the neighboring isles had come to Ulysses' palace, hoping to marry Penelope. For months and years they had stayed at her palace, feasting and drinking at her expense and demanding that she marry one of them. She told them that she could not wed until she had finished a shroud for her father-in-law, who was old and likely to die. She had spent years in making that shroud and even yet it was not finished,—for every night she had undone what she had woven during the day.

The suitors at last discovered the trick that Penelope was playing and refused to be put off any longer. They insisted that she must choose one of them for her husband. It was while they were doing this that Ulysses reached home.

ULYSSES

He planned a way to punish the suitors. He first sent Telemachus to the palace alone to see his mother. Then, dressed as a beggar, Ulysses followed with the swineherd.

When he came to the palace gate in rags and tatters no one imagined who he was, but his old dog Argo knew him and licked his hand. The swineherd led the way into the banquet hall, and a few paces behind him walked the ragged beggar, leaning upon a staff.

The swineherd kindly gave him a seat and invited him to eat and drink of the good cheer on the table. Hardly had Ulysses seated himself when jests and insults were heaped upon him by the suitors. It wrung the heart of Telemachus to see his father so badly used in his own palace, but he kept his temper and waited.

Not long after Ulysses' arrival Penelope entered the banquet hall. She did not know that her husband had returned, but Minerva had told her what to do. So she stood beside one of the columns that upheld the roof of the hall, and said:

"Hear, all who are in this hall of Ulysses! You wish to take the place of my husband. I bring to you his bow. Whoever among you can bend and string it and with it shoot an arrow through twelve rings, him will I wed and him will I follow from this fair home."

Then the suitors, one by one, haughtily tried to string the bow. And, one by one, they utterly failed to bend it.

Ulysses then demanded that he, too, might try to bend the bow. Amid sneers and laughter he was at length allowed to do so.

As easily as a skillful player stretches a cord from side to side of the harp, so without any effort he strung the bow; and forthwith through each and all of the twelve rings an arrow winged its way. It was followed by another which struck the chief man among the suitors dead. Telemachus and two faithful men, who had already locked the doors of the hall, now lent their aid to Ulysses. Arrows flew, swords flashed, and clubs were swung, until all the suitors who had tried to steal his wife and kingdom from Ulysses lay dead on the floor of the banquet hall.

Penelope's joy was great when she learned that the beggar was her husband; and Ulysses' delight at finding that she still loved him made all his weary wanderings seem like a dream.

ULYSSES SLAYS THE SUITORS

41

Chapter 11

Lycurgus

PART I

ABOUT eighty years after the Trojan War the descendants of Hercules with a large band of followers invaded the Peloponnesus, or southern part of Greece, where Agamemnon and Menelaus had once lived. They captured Sparta and made it their capital and after that called themselves Spartans.

The Spartans made slaves of people who were already living in the country and called them Helots or captives. The conquerors divided the land among themselves and made the Helots work their farms.

After about three hundred years had passed it seems that some of the Spartans had grown rich, while others had lost their land and slaves and become poor.

The Spartans who had lost their property were not willing to work like the slaves, and sometimes, when they had no bread for their children, bands of them marched through the streets of Sparta, broke into the houses of the rich and took whatever they could lay their hands on.

During one of these riots, one of the two kings,—for the Spartans always had two kings with equal power,—went out of his palace to stop it. He tried to persuade the people to go quietly home, but they paid no attention to him and a butcher in the crowd rushed up and stabbed him.

The murdered king left two sons. The elder became king, but soon died. The younger was one of the wisest and best men that ever lived in Greece. His name was Lycurgus and after his brother's death every one wished him to become king. But an infant child of the late king was the rightful heir, and Lycurgus refused to be anything more than regent.

For a while he ruled in the young king's name, but some people accused him of wishing to make himself king. So he gave up the regency and went traveling. He visited many lands and studied their plans of government. After being absent several years he came back to Sparta. There he found that the rich were richer and the poor were poorer and more unhappy than when he went away. Everyone turned to him as the only man from whom help could come.

He persuaded the people to let him make new laws for Sparta. The first change that he made was to give every Spartan a vote. There was a Senate of Thirty which might propose laws, but all the citizens were called together to pass or reject them.

Next he persuaded the rich people to divide their land fairly among all the citizens. So now no one had more than he needed, but every one had a farm large enough to raise wheat or barley, olive oil and wine for his family for a year. No Spartan was permitted to work or to engage in any trade, but the slaves were divided, so that every Spartan had slaves to work for him.

Besides the Spartans and the slaves there was another class of men living on the lands of Sparta who were not slaves like the Helots, and yet not citizens like the Spartans. These men were farmers, traders and mechanics. They had to pay taxes and fight when called upon, but neither they nor the Helots had anything to say about the government. There were about , pure Spartans and about , in the two lower classes, so you will see that the political power in Sparta was in the hands of a very few men. Their government was what we call an "oligarchy," which means a government by the few.

PART II

LYCURGUS did not wish the Spartans to become traders and grow rich, and it is said that he ordered their money to be made of iron. This iron money was worthless outside of Sparta, so the traders of other countries would not take it in payment for their goods and sold nothing to Spartans.

In those days soldiers fought chiefly with swords and spears; therefore no matter how brave men were, they had to have physical strength to win a victory. Lycurgus made laws that the men and boys of Sparta should be trained in running, boxing, wrestling, throwing quoits, hurling javelins, and shooting with bows and arrows. The girls had nearly the same training.

GREEK GIRLS PLAYING BALL

The feeble and deformed were thought by Lycurgus to be useless. Infants were therefore examined and those that were weak or deformed were not allowed to live. A strong, well-formed infant was handed back to its parents with the order, "Bring up this child for Sparta."

Boys remained at home until they were seven years old. Then they were taken in charge by the State to be trained. The clothing given them was scanty. They went about with their heads and feet bare, and slept on hard beds, or even on floors, with rushes instead of a mattress.

To teach the boys temperance Helots were sometimes purposely made drunk. Thus the boys saw how foolish men become when they drink too much.

One lesson that every Spartan boy had to learn was to endure pain without flinching. Another was that in battle a man might die, but must not surrender. When the young Spartan was leaving home for the field of battle his mother would hand him his shield and say, "Come back with this, or upon this."

YOUNG SPARTANS LEARNING A LESSON FROM DRUNKEN HELOTS

Lycurgus was opposed to all expensive ways of living. He thought that luxury was a waste of money and made men weak and effeminate. He made a law that the men should not take their meals at home but in a public dining hall; and there only the simplest kind of food was set before them—bread, cheese, olive oil, and a kind of black broth that was probably made of black beans. Figs and grapes served for dessert. It is said that some rich people were very angry because they had to eat at the public tables and that one young man stoned Lycurgus.

A great change came over the Spartans after they had adopted the new laws and ways of living. Instead of being a nation of idlers they became so strong and brave that when there was talk of building a wall round the city, Lycurgus said, "Sparta's citizens are her walls."

When Lycurgus saw what improvement had been made he told the people that he was going on a long journey. He made them promise that they would not change his laws until he returned.

He never returned. When the Spartans felt sure that he was dead they built a temple in his honor and worshiped him as a god. He left Sparta about B.C. and his laws were not changed for several hundred years. They made Sparta the greatest military state in Greece.

Chapter 12

Draco and Solon

PART I

ONE of the first Athenians whose doings belong to history is Draco, who lived about years before Christ.

At that time the working people of Athens were very unhappy. One reason of this was that the laws were not written and the judges were very unfair. They almost always decided in favor of their rich friends. At last everybody in Athens agreed that the laws ought to be written out and Draco was asked to write them.

Some old laws were so severe that often people had been put to death for very slight offences. Draco changed these severe laws and made new ones a great deal more merciful, and this made the people very fond of him. A story is told about his death which shows that other people besides the Athenians thought a great deal of him. He went to a theater on an island not far from Athens, and when the audience in the theater saw him they threw to him their cloaks and caps to do him honor. Unfortunately, such a pile of cloaks fell on him that he was smothered to death.

Even after the laws had been written the people were not happy, because Draco had not changed some laws that bore very hard upon the poor. These were the laws about debts. If a man borrowed money and could not pay it back at the right time, the man who lent the money might take the borrower's house and farm and might even sell him and his wife and children as slaves. On most of the farms near Athens stone pillars were set up, each of which told that the land on which it stood was mortgaged, or pledged, for a debt. Many of the farmers and their families had been sold as slaves. In time it came to be said that Draco's laws were written in blood.

PART II

HAPPILY, a very wise and good man called Solon was then living in Athens, and the Athenians asked him to make a new set of laws.

Rich and poor were surprised when they read Solon's new laws. The poor who had lost their farms and houses were to have everything given back to them. Solon thought they had paid so much interest for so many years that their debts should be forgiven. All who had been sold as slaves were to have their

SOLON DEFENDS HIS LAWS

freedom and no one was ever again to be sold for debt. Those debtors who had not lost everything were to be forgiven about a quarter of what they owed.

AN ATHENIAN OF
OLDEN TIMES

All this Solon called a "shaking-off of burdens," and thousands of people felt that heavy burdens had indeed been taken from their shoulders.

Solon did another good thing for the people. He gave every citizen a vote and all could attend the Assembly of the people, which was like a New England town-meeting.

There was a Senate of Four Hundred, which proposed laws, but the people themselves met and passed them. So the people of Athens really made their own laws.

Besides this, the Assembly chose every year nine archons, as the rulers of Athens were called. The chief archon was like the mayor of one of our cities and the others like the aldermen. Under Solon's new laws Athens soon came to stand in Greece for government by all the people, just as Sparta stood for government by the few.

PART III

WHEN Solon saw that his laws were making the Athenians contented and prosperous, he made them promise not to change them for ten years. He then went on a long journey.

One of the countries which he visited was Lydia in Asia Minor. Crœsus, the king of Lydia, was called the richest man in the world. He was so famed for his wealth that even now you often hear people say that a man is "as rich as Crœsus."

Crœsus was very proud of being so rich and wished Solon to flatter him. So he asked Solon, "Who is the happiest man you have ever known?" He expected the Athenian of course to say, "Yourself, your Majesty."

Solon however replied, "An Athenian peasant who never suffered want, who had a good wife and children, and who died on the battlefield for his country."

"Who is the next happiest?" asked Crœsus.

"The two next happiest persons whom I have known," said Solon, "were the sons of a certain priestess of Juno. It was her duty to offer a sacrifice in the temple. When the time came for her to go the oxen to draw the cart could not be found. So her sons yoked themselves to the ox-cart and drew her all the way to the temple. She was so much pleased at them that she prayed to Juno to grant her sons the greatest blessing that they could have. The mother's prayer was answered, for the sons lay down to sleep in the temple and never waked. They had done their parts well in the world and they left it without pain or sorrow, beloved and admired by all who knew them."

"But," cried Crœsus, "do you not think a rich and powerful king like me is happy?"

"Ah, Crœsus," said Solon, "I call no man happy until he is dead. You are rich; you are king of thousands of people; you live a life of luxury; but none of these things proves you happy. When I hear whether or not your life has ended nobly, then I shall know whether or not you were really happy."

Years afterward when Crœsus had lost his kingdom and his wealth, he saw how wise this speech of Solon was.

After ten years of travel Solon returned to Athens where he lived in honor until his death.

Chapter 13

Pisistratus the Tyrant

PART I

WHEN Solon came back from his travels he found that a young kinsman of his, named Pisistratus, was trying to make himself master of Athens. Pisistratus was rich and gave away a great deal of money, and in every possible way showed himself friendly to the people. His

IN A GREEK HOME

large and beautiful garden was thrown open to them, as if it were a park. Men and women of the working-classes were allowed to sit under his shade trees and their children played among his flowers. When the poor were ill he had nice things cooked for them in his own kitchen, and often in the heat of summer he sent to the sick a present of snow, which was a rare luxury. If a poor man died Pisistratus often paid the expense of burying him. Poor people in Athens were very much pleased by this, because they believed that if a person were not properly buried his soul would have to wander a hundred years up and down the bank of the river Styx.

One day, after the kindness of Pisistratus had made him the idol of the Athenians, he drove his chariot rapidly into the market-place. A crowd immediately gathered about him, for they saw that something was the matter. In a state of great excitement he showed some wounds,—which he had really made upon himself, but which he pretended he had received while he was driving along the high road.

"Men of Athens!" he cried, "See what my enemies have done to me because I am a friend of the people." All saw the blood on his face and of course believed what he said. They were very angry, and one of them proposed in the public Assembly that in future fifty men, armed with clubs, should be paid by the State to guard Pisistratus.

Solon begged the people to vote against this. But they had made up their minds and Solon could not dissuade them. The guard was ordered, and Pisistratus took good care that there should be in it a great many more than fifty men. Very soon he had a company of soldiers who were ready to do whatever he ordered. So, just as Solon had feared, he seized the Acropolis, a high, rocky hill which was the citadel of Athens, and made himself master of the city.

After a while the people grew tired of him and he had to leave Athens. However, he came back and regained his power by playing a trick on the people. A very tall and beautiful girl, in full armor, rode into the city standing at his side in a chariot. Minerva herself was said to be bringing Pisistratus back. When the chariot came into view the people shouted with joy and welcomed their old friend.

Soon he was banished a second time, but again recovered his power, and from that day to the time of his death he had full sway over the city.

PART II

ALL the states of Greece had in time become republics, except Sparta, and when anyone took the power of a king in any of these states he was called a tyrant. Thus Pisistratus was called the Tyrant of Athens, and yet he was by no means so harsh a ruler as the world might lead us to think. But he was strict. When he got control of Athens it was full of lazy people who lounged all day about the market-place. Pisistratus put all such people to work upon the roads or public buildings.

There were no public schools or libraries in Athens, but Pisistratus did his best to give the people a chance to read and to educate themselves. Books in his days were not printed, but written, and they were so expensive that few people could buy them. Pisistratus had a large collection and he invited all persons, rich or poor, to go to his library and read.

He did another thing for which the Greeks were grateful. For more than two hundred years before his time the poems of Homer had been recited all over Greece. Traveling minstrels sang them before guests in banquet halls, or before public gatherings. Every one loved these poems, and many people knew parts of them by heart. Pisistratus employed learned men to help him write them and put them in proper order. The verses about the Trojan War were arranged to make up the poem called the Iliad, and those about the wanderings of Ulysses to make up the poem called the Odyssey.

A READING FROM HOMER

Athens never had a wiser or better ruler than Pisistratus. He died B.C.

Chapter 14

Miltiades the Hero of Marathon

PART I

AFTER Pisistratus died his two sons, Hippias and Hipparchus, ruled over Athens. They governed well until Hipparchus was killed by his enemies. Then Hippias became so cruel that the Athenians banded together and drove him out of the city.

Some time after being driven from Athens Hippias sailed to Asia and begged Darius, king of Persia, to help him regain his power. At that time Persia was the greatest country in the world. Darius, her sovereign, was called "the Great King," or simply "the King," as if there were no other king on the face of the earth. He intended that there should be no other if he could have his way. He made up his mind not only to help Hippias, but also to make himself master of Greece. Persian heralds were therefore sent to every state of Greece to demand from each a tribute of earth and water. If the Greeks had yielded to this demand it would have been the same as saying that all the land and water of Greece belonged to Persia. Some of the states submitted, others proudly refused. The Athenians threw the heralds into a ditch into which the bodies of criminals were thrown; the Spartans threw them into a well and told them, "There you will find both earth and water for your master."

As soon as Darius heard of this he declared war and a little later his fleet, carrying one hundred and fifty thousand men, set sail for Greece. The Persians landed on the Grecian coast and went into camp on the plain of Marathon, twenty-two miles from Athens.

Meantime the Athenians had not been idle. They had collected a force of ten thousand men, and the entire army was under ten generals, each of whom in turn was commander-in-chief for one day. The little city of Platæa, unasked, had sent a thousand volunteers.

A SOLDIER OF ATHENS

The ablest of the Greek generals was Miltiades. He determined to attack the enemy at once, and when his day of command came, on the th of August, B.C., he drew up the Greek army in line of battle and moved across the plain. Then he charged upon the Persian army, broke their line, and drove them back to their ships in confusion.

News of the victory was carried to Athens by a soldier, who though wounded ran the twenty-two miles from the field of battle to the city. Reaching the market-place, he rushed into the crowd of citizens assembled there, and crying—"Rejoice! Rejoice! We are victors!"—fell dead.

This news delighted all loyal Athenians, but was very unwelcome to some traitors who had been hoping to hear of a Persian victory. These traitors had gone to a mountain near Athens, and with a polished shield they flashed to the Persian fleet a signal to sail to Athens and capture the city before Miltiades could return from Marathon.

GREEK CHARIOT

Fortunately, the signal was seen in the camp of the Greeks. Miltiades guessed what it meant and marched back to Athens immediately. So when the Persians approached in their ships they found that if they landed they must again meet the army of Miltiades. They had no wish to do this and sailed away across the Ægean Sea to the Great King's own dominions.

The battle of Marathon showed that the Greeks were equal to any soldiers in the world. They had routed an army of Persians fifteen times as large as their own, and had lost only one hundred and ninety-two men.

The Greeks believed that this splendid victory was won through the aid of their gods and of their god-like hero Theseus, who was said to have fought in the thick of the battle and made terrible havoc among the Persians.

PART II

MILTIADES won great fame in Athens. Honors were showered upon him and whatever he asked was granted. Thinking that he could add still more to his own glory and that of Athens, he asked that a fleet of seventy ships be placed at his command and that he be allowed to do with it as he pleased.

READY FOR BATTLE

The fleet was granted and with it he set sail for the island of Paros. The people of Paros had helped the Persians in the recent war and Miltiades wished to punish them, but he also hoped to avenge himself upon a personal enemy. The expedition was a complete failure. The town of Paros was not captured, and Miltiades was obliged to give up the siege and return to Athens.

Moreover at Paros his thigh had been badly hurt while he was leaping over a fence so that he came home injured as well as unsuccessful. Upon his return he was accused of having deceived the people and wasted the public money.

When his trial took place he was brought before his judges upon a couch, being too weak to stand or sit. The decision of the court was against him and he was sentenced to pay a heavy fine, which he was too poor to pay. Not long afterward he died of the injury that he had received at Paros.

After the death of Miltiades the Athenians were sorry for their harshness toward him. Remembering only his heroism at Marathon, they buried him with the highest honors on the plain where his great victory was won.

Chapter 15

Leonidas at Thermopylae

PART I

LEONIDAS was a son of one of the kings of Sparta. As a boy he was trained in the gymnasium and excelled in all manly sports. As a man he fought in the Spartan army. After the death of his father and his half-brother he became king. Eleven years later he led the Greek army against the Persians, who a second time were threatening Greece. The second invasion of the Persians came about in this way:

The defeat at Marathon had made Darius only the more determined to conquer the Greeks. But four years later, in the midst of his preparations, he died and Xerxes, his son, came to the throne.

Xerxes after a while decided to carry out his father's plans and spent four years in collecting men and horses and ships. His army and fleet were the largest that the world had ever heard of.

The land forces met at Sardis, a city in Asia Minor, and marched to the shore of the Hellespont, which you have already learned is the narrow strait between Europe and Asia. Xerxes ordered his en- gineers to make two bridges of boats across the strait for the passage of the army. This was done, but the bridges were not strong enough and a storm destroyed them. The loss of his bridges made the king very angry, and it is said that he had the strait scourged with three hundred lashes and a set of chains thrown into it, to teach the water that he was its master.

Two new bridges, stronger than the first, were built and Xerxes then marched his army over them to the European shore of the Hellespont. Here his fleet of twelve hundred war ships and three thousand smaller vessels had already arrived. On a hill overlooking the strait a throne of marble was built, and upon it Xerxes sat and reviewed his land forces drawn up along the shore, and his ships sailing in the strait. It took the army seven days and seven nights to cross the bridges.

After crossing, the land force made its way southward until it reached a high and almost impassable mountain range. Between this range and the sea the roadway at two points was so narrow that there was room for only a single wagon. There were hot sulphur springs near-by, and therefore the Greeks called this narrow part of the road Thermopylae, which means the "Gates of the Hot Springs." We usually speak of it as the "Pass of Thermopylae."

The Persians intended to march through the Pass, but they were stopped by a Greek force under Leonidas, king of Sparta. His band numbered only about four thousand men, of whom three hundred were Spartans, the rest being from several different states.

The Greeks took their stand at the narrowest part of the Pass. Against them Xerxes sent one division of his army after another, but all were defeated and driven

THERMOPYLAE AS IT LOOKS TO-DAY

back. For two days the fighting went on with great loss to the Persians, while the Greeks lost hardly a man.

At last, when it seemed impossible to overpower the Greeks, a traitor showed a band of Persians a path that led over the mountain. This path was poorly defended by Greeks from one of the northern states. It was easily taken by the Persians, who then marched round behind Leonidas.

Leonidas learned of their approach in time to escape. Some of his army did retreat; but he, with three hundred Spartans and seven hundred men of Thespiæ, a little town some distance from Athens, refused to do so. Greece had trusted the Pass to them to hold and they preferred to die rather than leave their post. When some one said that the arrows of the Persians would come in such showers as to conceal the sun, one of the Spartans replied, "So much the better; we shall fight in the shade."

Leonidas was now penned in between two divisions of the Persian army, one at each end of the Pass. Instead of waiting to be attacked he led his men forward against the Persians. The Greeks fought desperately, but they had no chance against such vast numbers. All were slain save one man.

A monument was afterward raised to their memory. It bore the simple inscription, "Stranger, tell the Spartans that we lie here in obedience to their commands."

After the battle Xerxes marched to Athens. He found it almost deserted. All the Athenians had fled save a little band who held

THE CAPTURE OF THE ACROPOLIS   the Acropolis. They hurled rocks upon the attacking Persians and for a long time resisted them. At length however the Persians found a place where no guard had been stationed, because the rocky wall was so steep that it seemed impossible to scale it. Here they climbed up and rushed in upon the brave defenders.

The struggle was soon over. Some of the Athenians hurled themselves headlong down the rocky slopes. The rest were put to death and the city fell into the hands of the Persians, who plundered and burned it. Even the sacred olive tree, which had sprung up at Athene's touch, was burned to the ground.

Chapter 16

Themistocles

AT this time the leading man of Athens was a great statesman and soldier named Themistocles. Some years before when the news had come that Xerxes was collecting an army and intended to invade Greece, the Athenians sent messengers to Delphi to ask the oracle what they should do. Delphi was upon the side of Mount Parnassus, and there stood a temple of Apollo. It was built over the cleft in the rock which, you remember, Deucalion found long ago as he and Pyrrha were coming down the mountain after the flood.

In the inner chamber of the temple just over the cleft, was a three-legged stool called a tripod. When a person wished to consult the oracle the priestess, who was called the Pythia, took her seat on the tripod. In a few minutes her eyes would close and she would begin to talk. The words which she spoke were noted, and the Greeks believed that they were really the words of the god Apollo.

Her answer to the messengers from Athens was:

"When everything else in the land of Cecrops shall be taken Jupiter grants to Minerva that the wooden wall alone shall remain undestroyed, and it shall defend you and your children. Stand not to await the attack of horses and foot from Asia, but retire. You shall live to fight another day. And thou, O divine Salamis, shalt destroy the children of women!"

What do you think this strange answer meant? The Athenians were greatly puzzled by it.

Themistocles said that the "wooden wall" meant ships of war, and that the gods would save the people if they would leave their city and trust to their fleet when the enemy approached. He advised the Athenians to build more ships of war. The people at last came to believe him. Rich

THE PYTHIA ON THE TRIPOD

Athenians gave him money, and the people voted that the silver which was dug every year from the silver mines owned by the city should be used to pay for building ships of war. And thus by the time Xerxes began his march Athens had a fleet of two hundred ships of war. These vessels were gigantic rowboats, each having as many as a hundred and fifty oars. Each had also a mast with a single big sail, which was hoisted to help the rowers.

The capture of Thermopylae had given the Persians an open road to Athens, and so the women and children of the city and the men who were too old to fight had been sent away in merchant ships to places of safety. A few men stayed in Athens and defended the citadel, as you learned in the last chapter. The rest went out in the war ships with Themistocles to fight behind the "wooden wall."

PART II

THEMISTOCLES and the commanders of the fleets of the other Greek states took their vessels into the narrow strait of Salamis, which lay between the island of Salamis and the shore of Attica. Here the Persians followed them. Themistocles now wished the Greeks to give battle to the Persians, but the Spartan commander and the other Greek leaders were unwilling to risk a battle in the narrow strait. They proposed to retreat. Themistocles was determined, however, that a battle should be fought in the strait; so he sent word secretly to Xerxes that the Greek ships were going to try to get away and advised him to head them off. Xerxes was delighted to get this message, and during the night he sent a part of his fleet up the shore of Attica to the other end of the strait, so as to hem the Greek fleet in between two lines of Persian ships. Next morning the Greek leaders all saw that there was nothing

to do but fight, and at once their ships were drawn up in line of battle.

Xerxes' throne had been placed on a high cliff on the shore of Attica, so that he might look down upon the battle. When the sun rose he took his seat upon the throne. He was clothed in his royal robes and surrounded by the princes of his court. Below him were a thousand Persian war vessels, while close to the shore of the island lay three hundred and seventy-eight Greek vessels. It seemed an easy victory for the Persians. The Greeks rowed forward from the shore of Salamis, shouting the cry, "We fight for all." The Persians replied with their war cry, and the battle began. For a time the Persians had the advantage. But their ships were in the way of one another; those in the front could not go back, those in the rear could not come forward. The confusion became terrible. Ship after ship of the Persians sank, some of them rammed by the Greeks, others run down by their own allies. In all two hundred Persian vessels were destroyed and a great number captured, while the Greeks lost only forty.

XERXES WATCHING THE BATTLE OF SALAMIS

When Xerxes saw his thousand vessels sunk or captured or rowing away in flight, he determined to go back to Persia. He at once returned to northern Greece, where he left men in command of his brother-in-law, Mardonius. With the rest of his army he marched on to the Hellespont. Here he found that storms had destroyed his bridges, so that what was left of his army was carried across to the shore of Asia Minor in ships.

THE VICTORS OF SALAMIS

PART III

EVERYBODY in Greece now admitted that Themistocles had been right in his explanation of the oracle that the "wooden wall" would save the people. And "Salamis," as the oracle had said, "destroyed the sons of women"; but they were chiefly the sons of Persian, not Grecian women. The battle of Salamis brought fresh glory to Themistocles. After some years, however, he became unpopular and was banished from Athens. He stayed at Argos. Then the Spartans, who were his enemies, accused him of treason against Greece. Fearing that he could not get a fair trial at Athens he fled to Persia. The Persian king gave him three cities to support him, and in one of these he lived until his death in B.C.

Chapter 17

Aristides the Just

ARISTIDES was the rival of Themistocles. Themistocles was wise and brave, but selfish and fond of money. Aristides, too, was wise and brave, but he was also so honorable that the Athenians called him "the Just."

On one occasion he was acting as judge between two men. One of them had spoken unfairly of Aristides and the other came secretly to Aristides to tell him of it. "My friend," said Aristides, "tell me the wrong the man has done to you, not what he has done to me. It is not my cause that I am to decide, but yours."

Aristides opposed many plans that Themistocles wished to carry out, and so at length Themistocles determined to have him banished.

There was at Athens a curious way of getting rid of a citizen. Every year this question was put before the people: "Does the safety of the State require that any citizen shall be banished?" If it was decided that this was necessary the people were called upon to vote. No person's name was mentioned, but every citizen wrote on a small earthenware tablet the name of any man whom he thought dangerous to the state. The tablets were collected and counted, and if the name of any one man was written on as many as , tablets

ARISTIDES

he had to leave the city for ten years. Banishing people in this way was called "ostracism." We often use the word to-day. It comes from a Greek word meaning an earthenware tablet.

Themistocles and his friends persuaded many of the Athenians that Aristides was a dangerous citizen. So when a public meeting was being held the people were asked if they thought any citizen ought to be banished. No one mentioned Aristides' name, but Themistocles' friends said, "Let a vote be taken." While the vote was being cast a countryman who could not write his own name came up to Aristides and said:

"Friend, will you write the name of Aristides for me on this tablet?"

"Has Aristides ever wronged you?" asked Aristides gently.

"No," said the other, "I have never even seen him, but I am tired of hearing him called 'the Just.' " Aristides said no more, but wrote his own name on the tablet.

ARISTIDES
AND THE COUNTRYMAN

55

There were enough votes against Aristides to banish him. As he was leaving Athens he prayed the gods that the time might never come when his fellow-citizens should have cause to be sorry for what they had done.

That time came, however. Three years later when Athens was threatened by the Persians the citizens, at the request of Themistocles himself, recalled Aristides. He sailed from his place of exile to the bay of Salamis and went on board the ship of Themistocles only a few hours before the famous battle. Themistocles at once gave him command of one of the Athenian ships, and he did good service in the battle.

PART II

IN the spring following the battle of Salamis Mardonius, the Persian commander who was in Thessaly, tried to bribe the Athenians to become allies of the great king but they refused his offers with scorn. He then marched to Athens and the people abandoned the city, so that it fell into his hands.

The Greeks, however collected an army of one hundred and ten thousand men. Pausanias, a nephew of Leonidas, the hero of Thermopylae, was made commander-in-chief; but Aristides commanded the Athenian troops. Mardonius now retreated from Athens, destroying and burning as he went. The Greeks followed and overtook him near the city of Platæa, and there they defeated him in one of the "decisive battles of the world." Mardonius himself was killed.

It took ten days to divide the spoil and bury the dead. A tenth of the spoil was sent to Delphi and dedicated to Apollo, because the promise of his oracle that "the wooden wall would save the city" had led to the great victory of Salamis. A temple was erected to Minerva, and thank-offerings were made to other gods. "Liberty games" were established, to be held on the battlefield once in four years, and every year the tombs of those who had fallen in battle were to be decorated with flowers. The land upon which Platæa stood was declared to be sacred and the inhabitants of the city were to be always free from attack by other Greeks.

On the afternoon of the very day on which the battle of Platæa was won the Greek fleet gained a great victory over the Persians at Mycale, on the coast of Asia Minor. After their defeats at Marathon, at Platæa, and at Mycale, the Persians never again attempted to conquer Greece.

PART III

AS soon as the victory at Platæa had freed Greece from the ravaging Persian army, the Athenians flocked back to their ruined city and began to rebuild it. Aristides and Themistocles carried on this work hand-in-hand.

RUINS OF PLATÆA

It was found that the sacred olive tree on the Acropolis, though burned to the ground, was not killed. From its root had sprung a stout young shoot. This was taken by the citizens as a good omen and rebuilding of the city went on rapidly. The great sea-port called the Piræus was fortified, and a wall was built round the city.

These and other public works required a great outlay of money, and it was needful to put some one whom all the citizens trusted in charge of the fund raised. Aristides was chosen and enormous sums of money were placed in his hands. He used his office solely for the good of the people and never became rich. When he died, about B.C., the whole nation mourned and he was buried at public expense.

Chapter 18

Cimon

YOU remember that when Xerxes was preparing to invade Greece, Themistocles tried to get the Athenians to build ships and quit their city, and trust to the "wooden wall" of a fleet.

One day, while the people were still in doubt about what they should do, a tall and handsome young man, with a bridle in his hand, was seen hurrying through the streets of Athens toward the Acropolis. He entered the temple of Minerva, hung up his bridle as an offering to the goddess, and took down from the walls a shield. He prayed to the goddess and then carried the shield through the streets of Athens to the Piræus.

The young man was named Cimon. He was the son of the famous Miltiades and belonged to a class of Athenians called knights, who fought on horseback. For him to hang up his bridle in the temple was as much as to say that Athens now had no need of horsemen, but of seamen, as Themistocles was urging.

People were fond of young Cimon because of his pleasant ways, and when they saw that he thought well of Themistocles' advice a great many who had not liked it changed their minds.

Cimon himself sailed in the Athenian fleet and fought bravely in the battle of Salamis. He distinguished himself so much that not long after the Persians had been driven from Greece he was elected admiral of the fleet.

At that time there were a number of pirates living on the island of Scyros, in the Ægean Sea. They captured the merchant vessels that carried on the trade of the Mediterranean. Cimon took possession of their island and made the Ægean Sea safe for traders.

The island was the one on which Thetis had tried to hide Achilles when the Trojan War began, and somewhere upon it Theseus, the great hero of Athens, had been buried. Cimon made a search for the burial place and found it. He took the bones out of the tomb and carried them to Athens.

When he arrived at Athens and told that he had brought the bones of Theseus the whole city was filled with rejoicing. Games were held and theatrical exhibitions given. The great poets Æschylus and Sophocles wrote plays for the occasion.

Cimon took so much booty from pirates that after a while he became very wealthy. He was also very generous. His fine gardens were open to the public and people were allowed to gather fruit in his orchard. The Athenians said, "He got riches so that he could use them and then used them so that he got honor." His fellow-citizens almost worshiped him.

A GARDEN OF ANCIENT GREECE

PART II

AFTER some years of fighting the allies of Athens grew tired of warfare. So Cimon agreed to let them furnish ships and money, and he hired seamen and marines from among the Athenians, so that though the fleet was in name the fleet of Greece, it was really Athenian. He drilled his men well in naval warfare and took them on one expedition after another. Thus they became the finest sea-soldiers in Greece.

At one time Cimon learned that there was a Per- sian fleet off the coast of Asia Minor. Immediately two hundred ships were made ready and he sailed to attack the Persians. They had about twice as many ships as he had, but the Greeks destroyed a great number of the Persian vessels and captured two hundred.

THE GENEROSITY OF CIMON

Cimon then disembarked his men and fought a Persian army on land. He completely defeated it and so gained two victories in one day. Immediately after this he was told that another Persian fleet was not far off, and at once he sailed to the spot and destroyed or captured all the ships and the men upon them.

The Persian king was now glad to make peace. He agreed that no army of his should ever go nearer to the Ægean Sea than a day's journey on horseback—about fifty miles—and that none of his war-ships should ever sail near Greece.

The spoil taken on Cimon's great expedition was immense. It sold for so much that the Athenians took part of the money to pay for building the foundations of the great walls called the "Long Walls." These were to connect Athens with her ports and serve also as fortifications. Cimon paid for part of this work out of his own share of the spoils.

It seems strange that the Athenians should ever have turned against Cimon after all his victories. Yet they did. The reason was this:

A terrible earthquake happened in Sparta. The whole city was ruined and only five houses stood unharmed after the shock. One large building fell upon some of the young men and boys who were drilling and killed them.

While everything was in confusion and everybody was filled with alarm, the Helots flocked together from the fields, intending to massacre their masters. Fortunately, one of the kings heard in time that the Helots were arming themselves. He at once ordered an alarm to be given by sounding trumpets, and the Spartans seized their shields and spears and gathered together. When the Helots reached the city and saw the citizens ready to resist them they went back into the country.

But they had a large and powerful army and they persuaded some neighbors of the Spartans to join them. Then they seized a strong fortress near Sparta.

The Spartans were now in a dreadful plight. Their homes were in ruins, their slaves in revolt, and their neighbors aiding the slaves.

In their distress they sent to the Athenians for aid. The great comic poet Aristophanes says, "There was a wonderful difference between the scarlet robe and the white cheeks of the Spartan who came to ask us for troops."

Some of the Athenians advised that none should be sent. They thought it would be a good thing for Athens if Sparta lost her power, for the two cities were rivals. But Cimon persuaded his countrymen to send a large force. He said, "Athens and Sparta are the two legs of Greece. Do not suffer Greece to be maimed and Athens to lose her companion."

So Athenian soldiers went in command of Cimon and fought for the Spartans. But the Helots and their allies were too strong. The fortress was not taken. Then the Spartans suspected that the Athenians had not done their best and they said that they wished no more Athenian help.

This made the people of Athens very angry. They were enraged not only with the Spartans but with Cimon. They declared that any friend of Sparta was an enemy of Athens, and so they banished Cimon.

PART III

AFTER the Spartans had conquered their slaves they sent an army to attack Athens. A battle was fought not far from the city and the Spartans gained the victory.

Then some one was needed in Athens who could either beat the Spartans or make friends of them. Cimon was therefore recalled from banishment. Not long after his return he made a truce with the Spartans which lasted for several years.

Cimon thought that the best way to keep peace in Greece was to fight the Persians. So he fitted out a fleet and set sail from Athens to attack parts of the "Great King's" dominions.

He really hoped to overthrow the whole Persian empire. Before making any attack he sent friends to the oracle of Jupiter. The god refused to answer the question that they put and gave as a reason, "Because Cimon is already with me." The messengers wondered what this could mean, but when they reached the Greek fleet they found that Cimon was dead.

Some say he died of sickness, others of a wound which he had received while besieging a city.

Before he died he ordered his officers to conceal his death from the soldiers and to carry his body to Athens. This they did.

Chapter 19

Pericles

CIMON had a rival named Pericles who was the most able leader Athens ever had. He had the power of a tyrant but he used it for the welfare of the people.

A GREEK THEATER RESTORED

He had many excellent laws passed. One was that a man accused of any crime should be tried by a certain number of his fellow-citizens. This was like our trial by jury, and it gave an Athenian the same rights in a trial that an American citizen has to-day. Another good law proposed by Pericles was that any citizen who fought in the army or navy of Athens should be paid for doing so. Still another of his laws was that if a poor man wished to go to the theater he might get the money from the city treasurer to pay for his seat. You will remember that Themistocles and Aristides began to rebuild and beautify Athens after it had been burned by the Persians. This work was afterward carried on by Pericles. It was said that he found the city of brick and left it of marble.

Under his orders the white marble Parthenon, or temple of Minerva, was erected on the Acropolis. It was one of the most beautiful buildings in the world. In front of it stood a bronze statue of Minerva, so large that it could be seen far out at sea. Within was a splendid statue of the goddess, nearly thirty feet high, which was of ivory and gold.

Pericles made Athens strong as well as beautiful. He finished the "Long Walls" which Cimon had begun. These walls were built from the city to her ports, which were about four miles away. Between two of the walls was a roadway, by which in time of war provisions could be safely carried from the harbor to the city.

Sparta was not pleased to hear of the fortifications of her rival. Athens might make herself beautiful if she chose, but she must not make herself strong. The Spartans watched for an opportunity to quarrel with the Athenians, and the opportunity soon came. The people of Corcyra, an island now called Corfu, lying off the west coast of Greece, went to war with the people of Corinth. Athens helped the Corcyreans; Sparta, the Corinthians.

This was the beginning of a contest between Sparta and Athens which desolated Greece for twenty-seven years (B.C. to B.C.) It is called the Peloponnesian War, because most of the states in the Peloponnesus took part in it and were allies of Sparta. Athens also had her allies.

INSIDE THE
PARTHENON

Athens was well prepared for war. She had a large sum of money in her treasury, a good fleet, and about thirty thousand soldiers whom she could put into the field.

The Spartans brought a force of sixty thousand men into Attica to attack Athens. Pericles then urged the country people to leave their farms and homes and come into the city. They took his advice, and every vacant spot in Athens was filled with huts and tents. Pericles thought that Athens, protected by the "Long Walls," could stand any siege.

In this he was right, for the Spartans made no headway; but very soon the Athenians were attacked by a foe far more terrible than the Spartans. This was "the plague." So many people were huddled together in the city that it was impossible to keep it clean and healthy. People began to sicken and die by dozens, then by hundreds. The Spartans, fearing that the plague might attack them, retreated across the Isthmus of Corinth into Peloponnesus.

While Athens was in this desperate condition Pericles acted most nobly. The plague carried off his eldest son, his sister, and many of his closest friends. Yet he went among the people, calming and cheering them, and attending faithfully to the affairs of the government. It was only when he laid the funeral wreath upon the lifeless body of his favorite son that he broke down and sobbed and shed a flood of tears.

While the Spartan army was threatening Athens, and when the plague came, many of the Athenians blamed Pericles. But when he was in sorrow all Athens showed him the greatest respect and affection.

Not long after the death of his son, he himself was stricken with a fatal illness. As he lay dying one of those at his bedside spoke of the good that he had done for Athens.

"What you praise in my life," he said, "has been due to fortune. I deserve no credit for it. That of which I am proudest is that no Athenian ever wore mourning because of anything done by me."

His death occurred in the third year of the Peloponnesian War. It was a sad blow to the Athenians, for he was the greatest of all their statesmen.

PART II

ONE of the friends of Pericles was Phidias, the sculptor who moulded the bronze figure of Minerva that stood in front of the Parthenon. He carved also the ivory and gold statue of the goddess that was inside the building.

His fame spread over all Greece, and he was invited to adorn the temple of Jupiter at Olympia. For this temple he made his masterpiece. It represented Jupiter seated upon his throne. The statue was so perfect that it was considered one of the wonders of the world.

When Phidias, after several years absence, returned to Athens he was persecuted by the enemies of Pericles, because he was known to be a friend of the great statesman. He was first accused of having stolen part of the gold which had been supplied by the city to decorate the statue of Minerva. Fortunately, when Phidias was working upon the statue Pericles had advised him to fasten the gold on in such a way that at any time it could be taken off and weighed. It was now removed and weighed and the weight was found to be exactly what it should be.

PERICLES VISITING THE
STUDIO OF PHIDIAS

Phidias was then charged with having insulted the goddess Minerva, because he had carved upon her shield a likeness of himself and one of Pericles. On this charge he was cast into prison to await trial. Before the day of trial came, however, the great sculptor was taken sick and died.

PART III

UNDER Pericles Athens was at the height of her glory, and the twenty-eight years during which he was at the head of Athenian affairs are known in history as "The Golden Age of Pericles." At no other time were there in Athens so many great painters, sculptors, writers, and philosophers.

IN THE GOLDEN AGE OF PERICLES

A celebrated historian who lived during the age of Pericles was Herodotus. He is called "the Father of History."

Another famous historian of those days was Thucydides, who wrote a history of the Peloponnesian War.

Chapter 20

Alcibiades

PART I

DURING the "Age of Pericles" a young man named Alcibiades attracted a great deal of attention in Athens. He was a kinsman of Pericles and was rich and handsome. But besides his money and his good looks there was another thing that made the people of Athens think a great deal of him. He had won the crown three times in the chariot races at the Olympic games.

OLYMPUC FOOT RACES

These games are said to have been established by Hercules. They consisted of boxing, wrestling, running, throwing the javelin, and racing with horses, and were held once in every four years in the valley of Olympia, in the little Greek state called Elis, which lay northwest of Sparta. They were so important that the Greeks reckoned time from the first Olympic games of which they had a written account as we reckon time from the birth of Christ. These games first took place in B.C. The four years from one celebration to another were called an "Olympiad."

None but Greeks might take part in the Olympic games, and while the contests were going on tens of thousands of Greeks from every part of Hellas watched and applauded. To win the prize in any of the contests was the greatest honor for which a Greek could hope. The victor's name and the name of his birthplace were called aloud by a herald, and before the vast assemblage he was crowned with a wreath of wild olive cut with a golden knife from a sacred grove said to have been planted by Hercules.

His victories in the Olympic games made Alcibiades the idol of the Athenians. The young men of Athens admired him so much that some of them dressed as he did and even imitated the lisp with which he talked. He was, in fact, the leader of Athenian fops.

Unfortunately, he had very bad faults. He was frivolous and thoughtless and, worst of all, he was not sincere.

AN EVENING REUNION IN ANCIENT GREECE

While talking with Socrates, the great philosopher, who was very fond of him, he could talk as if he were good or at least wished to be; but the next day he might be leading his companions into all kinds of mischief. Yet with all his faults he was a brilliant genius; even serious people admired him and often took his advice.

During the Peloponnesian War he persuaded the Athenians to undertake an expedition against the island of Sicily. He reminded them that Syracuse, the most important city of the island, was an ally of Sparta and an enemy to Athens. This was one reason he gave why the expedition should be undertaken. Another reason was the advantage that would come to Athens if she should add this fertile island to her possessions.

An old Athenian general named Nicias opposed the expedition, but Alcibiades had his way. Ships and men were made ready and were put under three commanders—Nicias, Alcibiades, and a man named Lamachus.

One morning, shortly before the fleet was to set sail, it was discovered that a shocking insult had been offered to one of the gods. Along the streets of Athens, along the country roads, and in front of the houses were busts of Mercury, who was the protector of travelers. Ears and noses had been chipped from these busts in the night. The Athenians were a very religious people, and this insult to the god filled them with terror. All feared that Mercury would punish them by not protecting people walking on the streets and highways.

Many thought that Alcibiades had chipped the busts for a frolic. Soon after the fleet reached Sicily orders were received that he should return to Athens at once to answer the charge. Of course he had to give up his command.

After he did so one disaster after another befell the expedition. The fleet entered the harbor of Syracuse. The Syracusans then blocked the entrance so that the Athenian ships could not get out. In the battle that followed half of Nicias' ships were destroyed. Nicias ran the rest ashore and tried to escape by land, but all were forced to surrender. The old commander was killed, and those of his men who did not die in battle or of starvation were sold into slavery. Not one of the ships of the fleet ever got back to Athens.

PART II

ALCIBIADES was either afraid that he could not clear himself, or that he could not get justice in the courts of Athens. He therefore pretended that he was going to obey the order for his return, but instead of doing so he went for refuge to Sparta. When the Athenians heard of this they passed a sentence of death upon him.

In Sparta he was warmly welcomed and by his pleasing ways became a general favorite. The Spartans, however, soon grew suspicious of him and ordered him to be put to death as a traitor to them. He managed to escape and went to Persia. Here again, as at Athens and at Sparta, he made the people fond of him. But after a while the Persian governor, who had been his best friend, saw that he was treacherous and put him in prison. He escaped and went to a place on the Hellespont where he joined the Athenian fleet. There he gave the commanders such advice that they gained a victory over the fleet of the Spartans and the land forces of the Persians. The Spartan admiral was killed. His successor wrote to Sparta, "Our glory is gone. The men are without food. We know not what to do."

Alcibiades now thought that he might venture to go back to Athens. As he had given to the com- manders of the Athenian navy the advice which won for them the victory over the Spartan fleet the Athenians repented of having condemned him to death. So when he arrived in the Piræus, with a small fleet of twenty vessels, he was allowed to land and go to Athens. In a very short time he persuaded the Athenians to give him command of their fleet. Then he sailed across the Ægean to fight against the Persians and Spartans.

Unfortunately, he had to leave the fleet for a short time. During his absence his lieutenant foolishly brought on a battle. The Athenians were defeated, and many of their ships were captured by the Spartans.

With what was left of his fleet Alcibiades then did the strangest thing possible; he attacked a city that was friendly to the Athenians and tried to make slaves of some of the inhabitants. Complaint was made of this to Athens, and the Athenians at once dismissed Alcibiades from the command of their fleet.

After this he lived for some years in Asia Minor, where he owned a castle. One night his castle was surrounded by armed men who set it on fire. He ran through the flames and tried to escape, but his enemies killed him (B.C. .)

Chapter 21

Lysander

THE admiral of the Spartan fleet in the last years of the Peloponnesian War was a man named Lysander. He was brave, but he was also cunning and frequently gained the victory by laying a trap for his enemy. It is said that he used to tell his officers, "When the lion's skin is too short you must patch it with that of a fox." This was another way of telling them that if they could not succeed by force they must try cunning.

After Alcibiades had been dismissed from the command of the Athenian fleet a commander named Konon was appointed to succeed him. Lysander decided to set a trap for him. The two fleets came in sight of each other off the shore of the Hellespont, near a place called Ægos Potamos, which means Goat's River. One morning, at break of day, Lysander drew up his ships in line as though he intended to give battle. Later in the day the Athenians rowed toward the Spartans and challenged them to fight, but not a Spartan vessel moved. The Athenians concluded from this that the Spartans were either not prepared to fight, or were afraid. The next day the challenge was again given by the Athenians, and again the Spartans paid no attention to it. The same thing happened the third day and the fourth. By this time the Athenians felt sure that Lysander was afraid of them. Many therefore went on the shore, some in search of provisions, some to take a stroll, some to sleep. Only a small guard was left with the fleet.

THE MARKET PLACE OF ATHENS

As soon as Lysander saw that the Athenians ships were unprotected he rowed swiftly to the place where they were lying and captured nearly the whole fleet. Of one hundred and eighty ships only about ten escaped. Three or four thousand men were taken prisoners, and all were put to death.

One of the vessels that escaped rowed direct to the Piræus to carry the terrible tidings. It arrived at night, and a sadder night was never known in Athens. The news spread through the city. Every house became a house of mourning. Nobody slept. All feared that Lysander would sail into the harbor with his victorious fleet. This was exactly what he did. All the seaports of Athens were blockaded by the Spartan vessels. The wheat supply was cut off, so that the people of the city were soon half starving.

The Athenians had now neither army nor fleet. After a three months' siege, during part of which time there was a severe famine, the city surrendered.

The only hope of the citizens was that their conquerors might be generous. But in this they were disappointed. The Spartans' terms were hard and cruel. One mile of each of the Long Walls was to be pulled down. Athens was to have no larger fleet than twelve ships of war. The Spartans were to name her rulers.

To wound the pride of Athens as much as possible Lysander had the long walls pulled down to the sound of music, and a part of the work was done on the anniversary of the battle of Salamis, a day always celebrated in Athens in memory of her great victory over the Persians.

Thus ended the Peloponnesian War (B.C.). It had been a fierce struggle, and all Greece had suffered. Thucydides, who wrote the history of this war, says that never had so many cities been made desolate, never had there been such scenes of slaughter.

Athens was ruined. She had lost her ships and her army, and she was helpless in the hands of Sparta. Thirty men were appointed by the Spartans to govern the city. They are known in history as the "Thirty Tyrants." Their rule was very harsh. They allowed only , Athenians to live in Athens. The rest of the people had to leave the city, and Sparta forbade all other Grecian cities to give them refuge. Thebes and Argos, however, boldly defied this cruel order, and many of the banished Athenians went to live in these cities.

RUINS OF THE LONG WALLS

After eight months the Athenians, under a leader named Thrasybulus, overthrew the "Tyrants." But in that short time no less than fourteen hundred Athenians citizens had been put to death.

Lysander's capture of Athens made him so popular in Sparta that for some years he was the real head of the government, and he made up his mind to seize the throne.

Before he could carry out his plans, however, he was put at the head of a Spartan force and sent to the city of Thebes, against which the Spartans had declared war. His army was routed by the Thebans and Lysander himself was among the slain.

Chapter 22

Socrates

SOCRATES

DURING the Peloponnesian War a very curious man lived in Athens. His name was Socrates. He must have been the ugliest person in all Greece. His nose was flat, his lips were thick, his eyes were bulging, and his face was like a comic mask; yet he was one of the best and wisest men that ever lived. His father was a sculptor who carved beautiful figures out of marble, and Socrates when a boy helped him and learned the art.

When the Spartans sent their armies to burn the farm-houses of Attica and capture cities that were friendly to Athens, many of the young men of the city went forth to fight for their country. Socrates laid down his hammer and chisel and took up a shield and spear instead. He fought in several battles, and Athens had no braver soldier. Once in winter he was ordered to a country called Thrace. It was very cold and "camping out" was not pleasant. However, Socrates bore the cold cheerfully, although he went barefoot and wore the same clothes that he wore in the warm weather in Athens.

After serving as a soldier for several years he left the army and went home to Athens. Here he became a teacher. He had no school-house. His school was wherever he met persons who were willing to listen to him. It might be in the market-place, or at the corner of streets. On a hot summer day he would go to the harbor of Athens and chat with people who were sitting there in the shade, enjoying the cool sea-breeze. He talked to the young as well as the old, and often he might be seen with a crowd of children about him. The lessons that he gave were simple talks about the best way of living, or what the Greeks called "philosophy."

Socrates was very unlike other teachers in Athens—and almost everywhere else—for he never made any charge for his teaching. This kept him poor. His clothes were often threadbare and shabby, and so were those of his wife Xanthippe. He cared nothing for this; but she did and it is said that she often scolded Socrates because he did nothing to make money, but idled away his time in talking. Once, when he was going out of the house to escape from a severe scolding, she threw a pitcher of water upon him. "I have often noticed, Xanthippe, that rain comes after thunder," said the philosopher.

No man ever had better friends than had Socrates. But no man ever had worse enemies. Some people disliked him because he used to ask them questions which they could not answer without admitting that they were very foolish in their way of living. Others said that he was teaching people not to worship Jupiter and Minerva and the other gods of Athens, and that he was misleading the young men of the city.

SOCRATES TEACHING YOUNG ALCIBIADES

One of his enemies was a poet called Aristophanes, who wrote the most humorous plays that were ever acted in Athens. In one of them a wild young man is one of the characters and Socrates is another. Aristophanes made it seem that the teachings of Socrates had caused the young man to become wild. The play did Socrates a great deal of harm, for many people came to believe that he really was advising young men to lead bad lives.

Yet one of the worst young men of Athens once said, "You think that I have no shame in me, but when I am with Socrates I am ashamed. He has only to speak and my tears flow."

ARISTOPHANES

Finally, the enemies of Socrates brought against him in the courts the charge of ruining young men and insulting the gods. He was tried and condemned to drink the deadly juice of a plant called hemlock. In Athens condemned persons were usually put to death by making them drink this poison.

No man ever behaved more grandly when unjustly condemned to die than did Socrates.

Before he left the court he said, "My judges, you go now to your homes—I to prison and to death. But which of the two is the better lot God only knows. It is very likely that death is our greatest blessing."

Generally a person condemned to death had to drink the poison the very next day after his trial. But a sacred ship had just sailed from Athens to Delos. This ship carried every year the offerings of the Athenians to Apollo, the chief god of the island, and it was a law in Athens that no person condemned to die should be put to death while she was on her voyage to and fro. So for thirty days Socrates was kept in prison. During that time his friends were allowed to go to see him. In the prison he talked to them just as he had done in the market-place or on the streets. Some of his friends told him how sorry they were that he should die innocent.

COMEDIANS WITH MASKS

"What!" said Socrates, "would you have me die guilty?"

On the return of the ship from Delos he was told to prepare himself for death. He invited his friends to come and be with him at the end. He took with them his last meal and was as cheerful during it as if it had been a feast.

One of his friends asked where he would like them to "bury him."

"Bury me?" he said. "You cannot bury Socrates. You can bury my body; you cannot put me into a grave."

THE DEATH OF SOCRATES

He spoke about death and the future life and said that death was only the end of sorrow and the beginning of a nobler life.

When the jailer came with the cup of poison Socrates drank it as cheerfully as if it had been a glass of wine. He walked about the cell as he was bidden and then, beginning to feel sleepy, lay down. Soon after this he ceased to breathe.

Plato, who was one of his pupils, says, "Thus died the man who was in death the noblest we have ever known—in life, the wisest and the best."

PART II

AFTER the death of Socrates (B.C.) his work was carried on by his pupil, Plato, who became one of the most famous philosophers of Greece. His lectures were given in the shade of the trees planted by Cimon in the Academy years before.

THE SCHOOL OF PLATO

Besides great philosophers Athens had some famous painters. Two of the most celebrated were Zeuxis and Parrhasius, who lived about B.C. They were rivals. Once they gave an exhibition of their paintings. Zeuxis exhibited a bunch of grapes which had such a natural look that birds came and pecked at them. The people exclaimed, "Astonishing! What can be finer than Zeuxis' grapes?"

Zeuxis proudly turned to his rival's picture. A purple curtain hung before it. "Draw aside your curtain, Parrhasius," he said, "and let us look at your picture."

The artist smiled, but did not move. Some one else stepped toward the curtain to draw it aside, and it was then discovered that the curtain was part of the painting.

"I yield," said Zeuxis. "It is easy to see who is the better artist. I have deceived birds. Parrhasius has deceived an artist."

It is said the Zeuxis died laughing at a funny picture that he had painted of an old woman.

Chapter 23

Xenophon

PART I

ONE day as Socrates was walking through a narrow street in Athens he met a young man who was remarkably handsome. Socrates stretched out his staff so that the young man had to stop.

"Where can bread be found?" asked the philosopher.

The young man's manner was modest and pleasing as he told Socrates where to buy bread.

"And where can wine be found?" asked the philosopher.

With the same pleasant manner the young man told Socrates where to get wine.

"And where can the good and the noble be found?" asked the philosopher.

The young man was puzzled and unable to answer.

"Follow me and learn," said the philosopher. The young man obeyed and from that time forward was the pupil and friend of Socrates. He was called Xenophon, a name that afterward became famous among the Greeks.

The king of Persia at that time was Artaxerxes. He had a younger brother named Cyrus, who was the governor of some provinces of Asia Minor, which belonged to Persia. Cyrus thought that he had a better right to the throne than Artaxerxes and he determined to seize it.

The Persians had helped the Spartans in the Peloponnesian War, and Cyrus had found out what splendid fighters the Greeks were. He knew, also, that many of them had become so used to fighting that they did not like a life of peace and were willing to fight for any one who would pay them. He decided, therefore, to get the Greeks to help him to fight for the throne of Persia, and he sent to several Greek states to invite soldiers to join him, promising them great rewards if he succeeded.

Xenophon had a friend who was going with Cyrus and who advised Xenophon to go too. Xenophon talked the matter over with Socrates who told him to ask the oracle at Delphi what to do. So Xenophon went to Delphi, but as he had made up his mind to go on the expedition he did not ask the oracle whether he should go or not. He only asked to what gods he should sacrifice before he set out. After sacrificing as the oracle advised he started for Sardis, in Asia Minor, and reached that city just in time to join the expedition.

DELPHI AS IT LOOKS TO-DAY

Eleven thousand Greeks from different states had entered the service of Cyrus; so that with his Persian forces, , strong, he had an army of , men. Xenophon was not a general, or even a soldier, in this army. He seems to have gone with his friend, hoping that some opening would be made for him.

There was a magnificent road from Sardis to Susa, Artaxerxes' capital. But even upon the best of roads an army of a hundred thousand men, most of whom were on foot, had to move slowly. Cyrus' troops went about fifteen miles a day, and it took them six months to reach a place called Cunaxa, about seventy miles from Babylon.

Here they found Artaxerxes at the head of an army of nearly a million men. The troops of the Persian king advanced with a great shout, thinking that the noise made by thousands of men shouting would terrify the Greeks. But the Greeks only raised their warcry—"Victory!"—and steadily advanced, overcoming everything that was opposed to them. Unfortunately, Cyrus went into the battle himself at the head of his Persian forces. Seeing his brother, he rushed forward, exclaiming, "I see the man," and wounded Artaxerxes with a javelin.

He himself, however, was quickly killed by the soldiers of Artaxerxes. As soon as their leader had fallen Cyrus' Persian soldiers lost heart and fled.

PART II

THE Greeks were now in a terrible plight. They were six months' march from Sardis and opposed by an army a hundred times the size of their own.

In the battle of Cunaxa they had so thoroughly beaten the Persians that Artaxerxes and his men were afraid of them and decided to get rid of them by treachery. The Persian commander-in-chief, Tissaphernes, therefore invited the Greek generals to a friendly meeting and promised to furnish them guides and provisions, so that they might return safely to Greece. The generals, never suspecting foul play, went to the Persian camp. There they were all put to death. The Greeks were now greatly alarmed. The night following the assassination of the generals was one of terror. Not a fire was lit, even for the cooking of the supper. All slept with arms at their sides while the sentries listened to catch the slightest sound.

Xenophon spent the night in thinking what was best to do. It was clear to him that some one must be chosen by the Greeks as their leader and that they all must stand by one another. He felt sure that if this were done there would be a good chance of getting home safely. In the morning he told his thoughts and hopes to others of the Greeks, who were greatly cheered by what he said. Although he had held no office in the army before, he was now made one of its generals.

The shortest way to get out of the kingdom of Persia was to go to the Euxine, now called the Black Sea, which lay many hundred miles to the north beyond rugged mountains. At one of the ports on the shore of that sea the Greeks hoped to find ships in which they might sail to Greece.

The march was at once begun. All sorts of hardships were met with. There were snow-storms and bitter north winds; it was sometimes hard to get enough food; the mountain tribes, through whose land the army had to march, were often unfriendly and rolled rocks down the mountain slopes upon the soldiers. At last, however, the shores of the Euxine were reached. The Greeks, since the murder of their generals, had marched for five months in an enemy's territory. They had drawn supplies from the country and had lost but few of their men. The retreat was in fact a victory.

XENOPHON'S FARM

Xenophon returned to Greece, but he did not go back to Athens. During some of the time that he had followed a soldier's fortune he had fought with the Spartans against Athens and the Athenians had passed a sentence of exile against him.

He went to Sparta, and soon afterward settled on an estate in Elis. "Xenophon's farm" is still pointed out to visitors to Greece. He passed about twenty years quietly in hunting, writing, and entertaining his friends with stories of his life as a soldier on faraway battlefields. om notes which he made he wrote a history called the Anabasis, or "March up," which is an account of Cyrus' march up to Babylon and of the retreat of the Greeks. Owing to political troubles Xenophon finally had to leave his pleasant home in Elis. He went to Corinth, where it is supposed that he died.

Chapter 24

Epaminondas and Pelopidas

PART I

IN the city of Thebes not long after the Peloponnesian War lived two young men whose names were Pelopidas and Epaminondas. Pelopidas was rich; Epaminondas was poor. Both were fond of athletics and manly sports, but Epaminondas found his chief pleasure in books. Both were brave men and true and they loved each other like brothers.

Once, when their city was an ally of Sparta, they were sent by Thebes as soldiers to help the Spartans in a war with their neighbors, the Arcadians. The young men were fighting side by side when their comrades gave way and fled. Closing their shields together, they bravely held their ground and tried to drive back the Arcadians. Pelopidas was wounded and fell. Epaminondas would not desert his friend. Although badly wounded, he held the Arcadians in check until help came and he and Pelopidas were rescued.

EPAMINONDAS RESCUES PELOPIDAS

In time Sparta became jealous of Thebes and tried to take away the liberty of her people. A few rich Thebans were willing to help Sparta do this in order that they might be made the rulers. One day they led a band of Spartan soldiers, who happened to be passing, into the Cadmea. This was the rocky citadel of Thebes, which rose above the city as did the Acropolis at Athens. The Cadmea had never been captured. But on that day the garrison was taking a holiday, for the citadel had been given up to the women, who were celebrating a festival of Ceres in it. So the Spartans easily took possession of it, and having once got it they held it for four years.

During that time the men who had betrayed the citadel into the hands of the Spartans ruled Thebes as tyrants. They put some of the Thebans to death and banished others. Over three hundred were sent away. Among them was Pelopidas. Epaminondas was so poor that the tyrants did not think him of any consequence and he was allowed to stay in Thebes. He used his influence to get the young Thebans to drill in order to make themselves superior to the Spartans in skill and strength.

PART II

THE exiles went to Athens. After living there for a few years Pelopidas determined to free his country, and he easily persuaded the other exiles and some Athenians to join in carrying out his plans.

When everything was ready the exiles left Athens. Twelve of them volunteered to get into Thebes and kill the tyrants. They disguised themselves as hunters, divided into four parties, and taking hounds with them, hunted through the fields around Thebes. As dusk came on they made their way into the city. It was a cold winter day, snow was beginning to fall and very few people were in the streets, so the exiles reached the house where all were to meet without being noticed. Twenty-six citizens joined them and all remained in the one house until near midnight.

A patriot who was in the plot had invited the tyrants to supper at his house. At the supper wine was served, and the tyrants drank freely. After the supper some of the patriots, dressed as women, were admitted to the banquet hall. As soon as they entered the room the guests greeted them warmly, but the supposed women at once threw off their veils, drew their swords and killed the tyrants.

Pelopidas, with another party, went to the houses of two of the tyrants who had refused the invitation to supper, and after a fight killed them. The patriots then went from house to house, calling on all the people to defend their homes. The Spartan soldiers in the Cadmea heard the noise and saw the lights, but were afraid to come out.

In the morning the other exiles with their friends from Athens came into the city, and all the citizens rose up in arms. The Spartan garrison gave up the Cadmea and Thebes was free.

PART II

SPARTA waited eight years before a chance came to punish the Thebans. Then war was declared, and an army of ten thousand Spartans marched against Thebes.

The Thebans also raised an army, and through the influence of Pelopidas Epaminondas was elected one of the chief captains. Pelopidas himself was captain of a famous "sacred band" of three hundred young men who had taken an oath to give their lives in defense of liberty.

The two armies met near a town called Leuctra. There Epaminondas gained a great victory, although his army was less than half as large as that of the Spartans.

Epaminondas and Pelopidas drilled the men of Thebes so that they were the best soldiers in all Greece, and Thebes helped other Greek cities become independent.

Pelopidas went to Thessaly to aid the people of that state against a tyrant who was trying to rule all Thessaly. The army of Pelopidas was not nearly so large as that of the tyrant, but Pelopidas was victorious. Unfortunately, however, he was killed in the battle.

The Thessalians begged the Thebans to allow them to bury the hero, and their request was granted.

PART III

THE death of Pelopidas was a sad blow to Epaminondas. However, he did not let his grief stand in the way of duty. Athens at this time had grown jealous of Thebes and had united with Sparta; so the armies of the two cities met the Thebans under Epaminondas in the year   B.C., near the town of Mantinea, where a long and fierce battle was fought. At length the Thebans were   victorious and the Spartans were driven from the field.

THE PLAIN OF MANTINEA
AS IT IS TO-DAY

The victory, however, was dearly bought. Just when the tide of battle was turning and the Spartan ranks were breaking Epaminondas received a wound in the breast from a spear. The shaft broke and the head remained fixed in the wound. Epaminondas was told by his physician that he would die as soon as the spear-head was removed. Those about him wept, and one lamented that he was dying without a child to keep his name alive.

"Leuctra and Mantinea," replied the hero, "are daughters who will keep my name alive."

When he was told that the victory was secure he cried, "I have lived long enough," and with his own hand drew the spear-head from his breast.

Thus passed away a man who stands out in Grecian history as a spotless hero—a soldier who never fought except for freedom, a man who lived only to do good.

Chapter 25

Philip of Macedonia

AFTER the death of Epaminondas Thebes soon lost the high place she had gained among the states of Greece. For a while no state held that place. Sparta was never powerful after her defeats at Leuctra and Mantinea, and although Athens had rebuilt her Long Walls she was not the strong power that she had once been.

A state, partly Greek and partly barbarian, lying far to the north, suddenly took the lead in the affairs of Greece. It was Macedonia.

The king of Macedonia had a brother named Philip who had spent a part of his youth in Thebes. He had seen Thebes become the greatest of Grecian states through the bravery and military skill of Epaminondas, and he determined to make his own state great.

The chance came to carry out his determination. The king of Macedonia was assassinated, and the brother who succeeded him was slain in battle. Philip's infant nephew was heir to the throne, and Philip became the guardian of the little king. In a short time the claims of his nephew had been set aside and Philip was on the throne of Macedonia.

Not long after he became king Philip was married to Olympias, a proud and beautiful woman, daughter of the king of Epirus. Philip had seen her for the first time at a feast of the god of wine. She and her maidens were dancing among garlands of vines and flowers. On the head of Olympias was an ivy crown and in her hand a staff twined with a vine branch. As she danced her wild beauty won the heart of Philip. He asked her hand in marriage and she became his wife.

A DANCE IN HONOR OF THE GOD OF WINE

Philip soon showed that he was a wise ruler. He treated hs people with fairness, and they became very fond of him.

One day, after he had been drinking, he was acting as a judge and gave a decision against a woman. His sentence seemed so unfair to her that she thought he was under the influence of liquor. "I appeal," she cried.

"I am the king. To whom do you appeal?" asked Philip.

"I appeal from Philip drunk to Philip sober," she replied. The next day Philip considered her case again and decided in her favor.

PART II

IT was, however, his skill as a soldier that most endeared Philip to his people. He knew that the Spartans had become the masters of Greece because every Spartan was a trained soldier, and he knew that Epaminondas had won his great battles because of the way in which he had arranged his men. Philip, therefore, had his army carefully drilled and in battle he arranged his soldiers in his famous "phalanx."

This phalanx consisted of a mass of men, sixteen deep. If there were , men the front rank had , standing side by side. Three feet behind these stood a second rank of ,. Behind the second rank stood a third line of , equally close, and so on until there was a solid body of men sixteen deep and a thousand wide. Every man bore a round shield, about two feet in diameter, and a spike or spear, twenty-one feet long. The shields were buckled to the left arm and were held close together. Before them bristled the spear-points like a hedge. Against these spear-points neither men nor horses could advance; and the charge of the phalanx broke down everything before it.

Athens and Thebes were finally aroused to action against Philip by the eloquence of Demosthenes, the great orator, who was constantly sounding a warning. An army was sent to oppose the Macedonian. Philip met this army at Chæronea, not far from Thebes, and there gained a great victory.

This put an end to the power of Athens and Thebes and made Philip master of all the states of Greece, except Sparta.

But Philip was wise and fair enough not to become a tyrant. He knew the history of Sparta. The military training of the Spartans had made them strong; their tyranny had made them weak, for no state of Greece was ever content to remain under Spartan rule. Philip, therefore, acted generously toward the conquered states. He let each manage its own affairs, while a General Council, like our Congress, managed matters in which all were concerned.

The first thing that Philip proposed to the Council of the States was that all Greece should make war against Persia. The members of the Council were delighted and Philip was invited to be the commander-in-chief of the expedition.

Preparations for the invasion of Persia had already begun when Philip's career was suddenly ended by an assassin who, at a wedding feast, plunged a sword into the body of the king and killed him.

Chapter 26

Alexander the Great

PART I

ALEXANDER, the son of Philip of Macedonia and Olympias, was born on the same night that the great temple of Diana at Ephesus, in Asia Minor, was burned. It is said that while the temple was burning sooth-sayers ran up and down the streets of Ephesus, crying out that the night had brought forth sad disaster to Asia. This was true of the birth of Alexander as well as of the burning of the temple.

Alexander was educated chiefly by the famous Greek philosopher, Aristotle. The young prince was an earnest pupil. It is said that he could recite the Iliad of Homer from beginning to end.

He excelled also in athletic sports. The horses of Thessaly, a state of Greece adjoining Macedonia, were famed for their speed and spirit. While Alexander was still a boy a fine Thessalian horse was offered to his father at a very high price. Philip wished to have the animal tried, but the horse was so wild that every one was afraid of him. Philip was about to send him away when Alexander offered to ride him. The king gave him permission. Alexander had noticed that the animal was afraid of his own shadow. He therefore seized the plunging horse and turned his head toward the sun, so that his shadow fell behind him. Then patting his neck and speaking gently to him, he leaped upon his back and soon completely tamed him.

ALEXANDER TAMES
BUCEPHALUS

The head of the horse was supposed to have some likeness to that of an ox, so he was called Bucephalus, or Oxhead. He became Alexander's favorite horse and carried his master through many a march and many a battle.

Alexander's ambition was shown at an early age. While he was yet a mere boy he made up his mind to conquer the world, and when he learned from Aristotle that there were many other worlds in the universe, he was greatly saddened by the thought that he had not yet conquered one.

As Philip went on making one conquest after another Alexander became alarmed. "Why," he cried one day, "my father will leave nothing for me to do!"

However, when he became king, he found enough to do. First of all there were other claimants to the throne besides himself. Some of them Alexander put to death. Others fled the country. He learned that Thebes and other Greek states were thinking of throwing off the Macedonian yoke. He therefore gathered a large army and marched to Thebes at the head of it. The Thebans were over-awed and submitted to him without resistance. The Athenians, in spite of Demosthenes' advice, sent a messenger to him while he was at Thebes, offering their submission. A little later the Greeks met in general council at Corinth and gave him, as they had given Philip, the command of the expedition that was to be undertaken against Persia. Sparta alone refused to agree in the vote.

Alexander returned to Macedonia and marched against some Thracian tribes in the northern part of his dominions. While he was subduing them a report of his death reached Greece, and Thebes again took up arms. Suddenly Alexander appeared in Greece with his victorious army. He took Thebes by assault and pulled to the ground every building in the city except the house once occupied by the famous poet Pindar. Six thousand of the inhabitants were put to death; a few escaped by flight and the rest were sold as slaves.

PART II

ALEXANDER now began to prepare for the great expedition against Persia, which had so long been planned. Soon his army was ready to march. It consisted of less than , men, but with these he boldly crossed the Hellespont.

He landed on the Asiatic coast not far from the site of ancient Troy. From the plain of Troy he marched to the river Granicus, on the bank of which he fought his first battle with the Persians.

The Persian army was completely routed, and its commander killed himself rather than face the disgrace of his defeat. The great city of Sardis, the stronghold of the Persians in western Asia Minor, now opened its gates to the conqueror.

The following spring Alexander advanced into the province of Phrygia. In a temple in the city of Gordium was kept the chariot of Gordius, once a famous Phrygian king. The yoke of the chariot was fastened to the pole by a knot of tough fibre. The knot was said to have been tied by Gordius himself. It was very puzzling. An oracle had declared that whoever should untie it would become the master of Asia. Instead of trying to untie it Alexander cut it with one stroke of his sword. The people of Asia Minor took this as an omen that he was to be their master and offered him but little resistance.

Beyond the mountains in south-eastern Asia Minor, the "Great King," Darius was waiting for the Greeks with an enormous army. He became impatient and crossed the mountains into Cilicia. A battle was fought at Issus, but the Persians were no match for the Greeks. The battle ended with overwhelming defeat to the army of Darius and he fled from the battle-field. He left not only his baggage and treasure, but his wife and mother and children, all of whom fell into Alexander's hands. These captives were treated with much respect and kindness by the conqueror.

THE FAMILY OF DARIUS
AT ALEXANDER'S FEET

Soon after the battle at Issus Damascus was captured. Alexander then moved against Tyre, a famous port of Syria, whose trade was with every land and whose merchants were princes. So great were the resources of the city that it withstood a siege of seven months; but at the end of that time it fell into Alexander's hand and thirty thousand of its citizens were captured and made slaves.

From Tyre Alexander marched toward Egypt. On the way he passed through the Holy Land. When he reached Jerusalem he was met by a friendly procession of priests and Levites, who came out from the gates of the city, with the high priest at their head, to bid the conqueror welcome.

Egypt, like the Holy Land, was won without a battle. The people were weary of Persian rule.

In Egypt Alexander did one of his wisest acts. He founded a city near the mouth of the Nile to be a great trading port. It is still called Alexandria after its founder. Another wise act on Alexander's part was to invite the Jews to settle in his new city. He saw that they were wonderful traders; and, as he expected, they made Alexandria a greater commercial city than Tyre.

In the spring of the year B.C. Alexander again set out in pursuit of Darius, who had now collected another large army.

In October, not far from a place called Arbela, in Persia, the forces of Darius and Alexander met in their last great battle. Darius had done everything he could to insure the defeat of the Greeks. His army was said to number a million men. One division of it had two hundred chariots, to the wheels of which scythes were attached. The scythes went round with the wheels and were expected to mow down the Greeks like grass. In another division of the army were fifteen trained elephants that were intended to rush wildly among the Greeks and trample them down.

But the scythe-armed chariots, the elephants, and the million men were alike unsuccessful. The vast host was completely routed, and Darius turned his chariot and fled.

From Arbela Alexander pushed on to Babylon, whose brazen gates were thrown open to him. Susa, another great city of the Empire, surrendered without resistance. Then, to make his conquest complete he marched on to Persepolis, the magnificent capital of Persia proper. This city, with its immense treasure of silver and gold, fell into his hands. Five thousand camels and ten thousand mule-carts carried away the spoils, the value of which is said to have been $,,.

Alexander pursued Darius, but before he overtook him the Great King was murdered by one of his own satraps. Alexander had the body buried with royal honors and punished the satrap with death.

The Empire of Persia now lay at Alexander's feet, and the work for which the expedition had set out was finished. The young king, however, had no desire to return to Macedonia. He had conquered the East, but the East had also conquered him. He had become a slave to its ways of living. His old simple Macedonian tastes had been laid aside and his life was given up to pleasure.

PART III

SOON, however, he undertook another conquest and at the head of his veteran soldiers advanced eastward into Bactria and added this province to his dominions. Among the Bactrian captives was a beautiful princess named Roxana, who became his bride.

Southeast of Persia lay India, a vast empire rich in gold and diamonds. Alexander desired to add it to his conquests.

Great mountain ranges enclose India on the north and northwest. Crossing these are passes, through which travelers from Central Asia must go to reach India.

Alexander went by the way of Khaiber Pass and marched steadily onward till he reached the river Hydaspes. Here an Indian king, named Porus, engaged him in battle. Porus proved to be the most desperate fighter Alexander had met with in all Asia. When the Indian was at length overpowered and captured and brought before the conqueror, Alexander asked him how he expected to be treated.

PORUS BEFORE ALEXANDER

"Like a king," replied Porus.

"That you certainly shall be," said Alexander. And so he was, for it was the habit of Alexander to treat honorably all whom he conquered.

On the bank of the River Hydaspes Alexander had the misfortune to lose his horse Bucephalus. At the place where the animal died the conqueror founded a city which he named Bucephala in honor of his favorite.

The conqueror was not able to go on with his Indian campaign. His soldiers were worn out with marching and fighting and insisted that they would go no farther, and so, much against his will, Alexander was obliged to lead them back to Persia.

The return march was one of great hardship. At the mouth of the Indus Alexander sent the fleet to sail along the coast and up the Persian Gulf, while he led the land forces toward Susa and Babylon. The army had to march through a country which was hot, dry and barren. The men suffered dreadfully and Alexander shared their sufferings.

Shortly after reaching Babylon he was attacked by a fever, which he had not the strength to resist.

Around his death-bed were gathered his generals. They asked him whom he wished to succeed him. He drew his signet ring from his finger and handed it to Perdiccas with the words, "To the strongest." A little later he had ceased to breathe.

THE DEATH OF ALEXANDER

Thus passed away one of the greatest soldiers the world has ever known. At the time of his death, B.C., he was only thirty-two years old. His victories had been won and his conquests had been made in the short space of twelve years.

Chapter 27

Demosthenes

DEMOSTHENES

IN the city of Athens about twenty-five years after the Peloponnesian War there lived a delicate boy named Demosthenes. His father was a manufacturer of swords and made a great deal of money. But when Demosthenes was only seven years old his father died. Guardians had charge of his property for ten years. They robbed the boy of part of his fortune and managed the rest so badly that Demosthenes could not go to school to the best teachers in Athens because he had not money enough to pay them.

One day, when he was sixteen years old, a great trial was going on at Athens and he strolled into the court. There were fifteen hundred and one dicasts or, as we call them, jurymen in their seats, and the court was crowded with citizens who, like Demosthenes, had gone in from curiosity. A lawyer named Callistratus was speaking. He did not finish his speech for nearly four hours. But no one left the court until he ceased to speak. Then hundreds of people went out and hurried home. Demosthenes waited to see the end. When each of the jurymen had thrown a voting pebble into a basket the clerk of the court counted the pebbles and told the result. Callistratus had won the case.

Demosthenes went home determined to become a lawyer and public speaker. In one year from that time he brought suit against his guardians, delivered four orations against them and won his case. He recovered a large part of the property which his father left to his mother and himself.

After this he entered public life, but the first time he made a speech in the public assembly it was a complete failure. He stammered and could not speak loud enough, and in trying to do so he made odd faces.

People laughed at him, and even his friends told him that he never could be a speaker, so he went home greatly cast down.

Then an actor who was a great friend of his family went to see him and encouraged him. He asked Demosthenes to read to him some passages of poetry. Then the actor recited the same passages. The verses now seemed to have new meaning and beauty. The actor pronounced the words as if he felt them. The tones of his voice were clear and pleasant and his gestures were graceful. Demosthenes was charmed.

"You can learn to speak just as well as I do," said the actor, "if you are willing to work patiently. Do not be discouraged, but conquer your difficulties."

"I will," said Demosthenes. And he did.

It is said that to improve his voice he spoke with stones in his mouth, and to become accustomed to the noise and confusion of the public assembly he went to the seashore and recited there amid the roar of the waves. To overcome his habit of lifting one shoulder above the other he suspended a sword so that the point would prick his shoulder as he raised it.

He built an underground room in which he could study without interruption and practice speaking without disturbing any one. He had one side of his head shaved so that he would be ashamed to leave this retreat. Then he remained there for months at a time engaged in study. One thing that he did while there was to copy eight times the speeches in the famous history of Thucydides. This was to teach him to use the most fitting language. Besides all this he took lessons of an excellent speaker named Isæus who taught declamation. In this way the awkward boy who had been laughed out of the assembly became in time the greatest orator of Athens.

IN ANCIENT GREECE

Not only was Demosthenes a graceful orator, but he was wise and patriotic. He soon acquired great influence in Athens and became one of the ten official orators.

At this time Philip of Macedon had organized a strong army and was beginning those conquests which in the end made him master of Greece. Demosthenes from the first regarded him with suspicion, but said nothing until convinced that Philip was threatening the liberty of Athens and of all Greece. Then he urged the Athenians to fight against Philip as their forefathers had fought against the Persians at Marathon, at Salamis and at Platæa. "Philip," he said, "is weak because he is selfish and unjust. He is strong only because he is energetic. Let us be equally energetic, and being unselfish and just, we shall triumph."

Philip's victory at Chæronea completely disheartened the Athenians, and Demosthenes had to use all the power of his eloquence to rouse them. In his speeches he showed how the success of Philip and the failure of Athens were not due to the advisers of the people or to the generals who led their army, but to the Athenians themselves. "You idle away your time," said he, "going into barbers' shops and asking what news to-day, while Philip is gathering forces with which to crush you and the rest of Greece with you."

Philip tried to bribe Demosthenes, but the orator was absolutely incorruptible, and to the end of his life he raised his voice and used his influence for the cause of freedom against both Philip and Alexander. He delivered twelve orations on this subject. Three of these orations were specially directed against Philip and are known as the "Philippics." They are so bitter in their denunciation of Philip that to-day any speech which is very bitter and severe against a man or a party is called a "Philippic."

The most famous speech that Demosthenes ever made was in defence of himself and is known as the speech "On the Crown." He had advised the Athenians to unite with the Thebans against Philip. His advice was followed, and a victory was won. The Athenians were so much pleased that it was proposed to crown Demosthenes with a golden wreath at one of the great festivals. Now this proposal had to be voted on by the people, and some of Demosthenes' enemies objected. If the people refused to vote the crown it would have meant disgrace for Demosthenes and so he was obliged to go before the assembly to speak in defence of himself and to show that his advice to his countrymen had been correct. It was true that the Athenians had not been able to destroy Philip's power, or free the states of Greece from his control; but, said Demosthenes, "I insist that even if it had been known beforehand to all the world that Philip would succeed and that we should fail, not even then ought Athens to have taken any other course if she had any regard for her own glory or for her past or for the ages to come." By this he meant that it was the duty of her people to fight for what they believed to be right even if in the very beginning they had known that they could not succeed.

Grander words than these never fell from human lips, and when the vote was taken the people decided that he should receive the crown.

PART II

WHEN news reached Athens of the murder of Philip, Demosthenes rejoiced and placed a wreath upon his head, as if he were at a feast. He even persuaded the Athenians to make a thank-offering to their gods.

Alexander soon placed the Greek cities at his mercy. Then he demanded that Demosthenes and eight other Athenian orators should be delivered up to be punished for treason. Demosthenes told the people of Athens the story of the wolf and the sheep.

"Once on a time," he said, "the shepherds agreed with the wolf that henceforth they should be friends. The wolf promised faithfully never again to attack the sheep. But he said he thought it would be only fair that the shepherds should cease to keep dogs. The shepherds agreed and gave up their dogs. Then the wolf ate up the sheep."

The Athenians knew what Demosthenes meant, and heeded the lesson. They kept their watchdogs, Demosthenes and the other orators, safely at home.

Alexander at length withdrew his demand and treated the Athenians with kindness. However, this did not win the favor of Demosthenes, who continued to oppose the Macedonians at every step.

After some years one of Alexander's satraps stole a large treasure, fled to Athens and begged for protection. Demosthenes was unjustly accused of helping him and was condemned to pay a fine. He could not pay it and so went into exile.

When Alexander died the orator returned to Athens. The Athenians sent a man-of war to bring him to the Piræus. The magistrates, the priests and all the citizens marched out to welcome him and escort him to the city.

Demosthenes now made a last effort to free Athens. But Macedonia was still strong, and Athens and those who loved her were weak. In a short time the demand was again made that the orators be given up to be punished and Demosthenes again had to flee for his life. He sought refuge in a temple of Poseidon on an island near the coast of Greece.

The sacredness of the temple ought to have protected him, but he was not allowed to escape. The captain of the soldiers who were sent to kill him told him that if he would come out of the temple he should be pardoned. Demosthenes knew well that this promise would be broken. He asked to be allowed a few moments in which to write a letter, and his request was granted. He wrote, and then placed the end of his writing-quill in his mouth. Those who were watching saw him grow pale. He tried to reach the door, but fell dead near the altar. He had taken poison which he had long carried in the end of his writing-quill, for he feared that if he ever fell into the hands of the Macedonians, he would die in prison, or by torture.

Chapter 28

Aristotle, Zeno, Diogenes and Apelles

PART I

WHILE Alexander was conquering the world, there lived in Athens a man whose work survived hundreds of years after the conqueror's empire fell to pieces. Indeed, it exists to-day. This man was Aristotle, the great philosopher, at one time Alexander's tutor.

After Alexander became king Aristotle went to Athens and established a school of philosophy. His fame grew and he was called "the man of wisdom." He spent much of his time in writing, and wrote about almost everything that men thought of in his time. Some of his works are studied in our colleges to-day.

Like all other great men of Greece, Aristotle had enemies. Some of them accused him of not having respect for the gods. He, therefore, fled from Athens in order, as he said, to keep the Athenians from sinning against philosophy by banishing him. He died in exile.

It is said that for about two hundred years after his death people did not know what had become of his writings. The men to whom they were left had buried them in an underground chamber for fear the king of Pergamos, who was very proud of his library, would get hold of them. When the manuscripts were at last found they could still be read.

ARISTOTLE LECTURING

For hundreds of years after that Aristotle's writings were more widely studied in Europe than almost any other books.

PART II

ANOTHER great philosopher who lived during the time of Alexander was Zeno. He was born in Cyprus, but came to Athens in his youth.

He gave his lectures in a porch, called in Greek a Stoa, from which he and his followers are called Stoics. He taught that men should live simply, and learn to be neither fond of pleasure nor cast down by sorrow. To-day we call people stoics who endure pain and misfortune without complaining.

PHILOSOPHERS OF ATHENS

One of Zeno's rivals was a philosopher named Epicurus. He founded a school in Athens and taught there for thirty-six years. His enemies accused him of teaching that pleasure was

DIOGENES IN HIS TUB

DIOGENES LOOKING
FOR A MAN

the only thing to live for, and many people still have this idea. We call a man an "epicure" who is very fond of high living. Epicurus, however, really used the word pleasure to mean peace of mind, not the mere satisfaction of eating and drinking. Both he and his pupils lived in a very simple way.

One of the oddest of the Greek philosophers was Diogenes. He used to stand in the public places of the city and ridicule the follies of his fellow-citizens. Because of this habit he and his disciples were called cynics, or growlers, from a Greek word which means dog. It is said that he lived in a tub.

Many stories are told of the curious doings and sayings of Diogenes. Once in broad daylight he walked through the streets of Athens carrying a lighted lantern.

"What are you about now, Diogenes?" asked one who met him.

"I am looking for a man," sneered Diogenes.

Once, when he was on a voyage, the ship in which he was sailing was captured by pirates. The passengers and crew were taken to Crete and sold as slaves. The auctioneer who was selling them asked Diogenes what he could do. "I can rule men," was the answer. "Sell me to some one who wishes a master."

When the great Council of the States of Greece honored Alexander by asking him to lead their forces against Persia, the young conqueror visited Diogenes. The philosopher was then living at Corinth, in the house of the man who had bought him as a slave. He was in the garden basking in the sun when Alexander visited him.

"Can I do anything to help you, Diogenes?" asked Alexander.

"Nothing, but get out of my sunshine," replied Diogenes.

As Alexander was leaving this man of few wants, he said, "If I were not Alexander, I should wish to be Diogenes." It was as though he had said, "If I were not going to conquer the world, I should like to have the power which Diogenes has to conquer self."

PART III

A NUMBER of celebrated painters lived during the reign of Alexander. The most famous was Apelles. Alexander would allow no one else to paint his portrait. Apelles had talent, but he became a great artist as much by his patient industry as by his talent. His motto was "Never a day without a line."

Once he painted a horse and exhibited it in a contest with some of his rivals who also had painted pictures of horses. He saw that the judges were not going to give the prize to his picture, so he requested that all the pictures should be shown to some horses. This was done, and the animals paid no more attention to the pictures of Apelles' rivals than they would have paid to blank boards, but when Apelles' horse was shown to them they neighed as though they had seen a friend.

Chapter 29

Ptolemy

ONE of Alexander's favorite generals was Ptolemy. In the division of the Empire Egypt was placed in his charge. Other parts of the Empire were intrusted to other generals. One had Macedonia, another Thrace, another Syria. At first they ruled as governors for Alexander's young son, but after a while they became independent and were called kings.

Ptolemy and his descendants ruled Egypt for more than three hundred and fifty years. They were a great line of sovereigns and did much for the good of the country. We are accustomed to think of them as Egyptians, but really they were Greeks living in Egypt.

One of Ptolemy's first acts, and one which shows that he was a man of affectionate feeling, was to bring the body of Alexander from Babylon to Egypt. It was first buried in Memphis but afterward removed to Alexandria, because, as you remember, this city was founded by Alexander and named after him.

Ptolemy made Alexandria his capital and did a great deal to beautify the city. He founded a museum and began collecting books for a library.

His son, Ptolemy Philadelphus, carried on this work and made the library the largest and best in the world. Most of the books were made of the pith of the papyrus or paper plant, of which you have read in the story of Pisistratus. They were written in Greek and Latin.

Ptolemy appreciated the intelligence and learning of the Jews and treated them with so much kindness and gave them so many liberties that great numbers of them settled in Egypt.

PTOLEMY PHILADELPHUS GIVES LIBERTY TO THE JEWS

Two things that Ptolemy Philadelphus did are especially worth remembering. One was to cause the Bible of the Jews to be translated into Greek; the other was to open again a great canal which had been dug many centuries before from the Nile to the Red Sea, but had long been filled up by the drifting sand of the desert. This was something like the cutting of the Suez Canal.

Ptolemy's canal connected the Atlantic with the Indian Ocean. Ships could sail from the Atlantic across the Mediterranean, then through the canal and the Red Sea, and on to India.

At that time Egypt raised more wheat than any other country in the world, so she had a great commerce. In exchange for her wheat she bought the products of Europe and Asia, and Alexandria became the richest city of the world.

But, more than that, the Ptolemies, especially Philadelphus, invited learned men to their court and gave them support so that they might carry on their own studies and teach others.

At one time there were , students receiving instruction in the city. Thus Alexandria became the home of learning. It was there that pupils were first taught that the earth is round, and one of the great astronomers who lived there found out very nearly the length of the earth's circumference and diameter.

The people of Alexandria knew more about these things two hundred years before Christ than the people of Europe did a thousand years after. The science of to-day about which you hear so much is only the continuation of what was begun by the wonderful Greeks whom the Ptolemies gathered about them in Alexandria.

One of the Ptolemy line was the celebrated Cleopatra, an able ruler and the most fascinating woman of her time. You will read something of her history in "Famous Men of Rome," a companion volume to this book.

Chapter 30

Pyrrhus

PART I

A PRINCE named Pyrrhus lived in the state of Epirus not far from the home of the great Achilles. At twelve years of age he became king, but the government was carried on for him by guardians.

About that time he read the story of Alexander the Great, and determined to be like him, a great conqueror. While he was dreaming of victories in foreign lands war came to him in his own country, and he was driven from Epirus. Ptolemy of Egypt helped him to defeat his enemies and regain his throne. Then he resolved anew to conquer as Alexander had conquered, and he began with Alexander's own Macedonia. After a war that lasted several years he got possession of one-half the country. One of Alexander's generals took the other half. However, the people in Pyrrhus' half preferred the old general as a ruler, and in seven months Pyrrhus had to give up his Macedonian kingdom.

He reigned quietly in Epirus for a few years. Then a chance came to try and conquer the Romans who lived just across the Adriatic Sea. Pyrrhus was delighted. Ruling Epirus was a dull business. In the south of Italy a great many Greeks had settled. Greek was the language of the people who lived there and the region was called "Great Greece."

Rome wished to rule all Italy, but those Greeks were not willing to be under Roman rule; so they sent word to Pyrrhus that they were in trouble and would like him to help them.

Preparations for war were at once made and as soon as possible Pyrrhus landed on the shores of Italy with an army of about , men and twenty elephants.

A great battle was fought, and Pyrrhus won the victory, but the loss of life was dreadful. As he walked among the dead after the battle he said, "Another such victory and I shall have to go home alone." Half his men were slain.

However, the Greeks of South Italy furnished him with fresh soldiers and he gained a second victory.

The war came to an end in a very curious way. One of the servants of Pyrrhus deserted to the Romans and offered to poison his master for the consuls. The consuls sent back the deserter to Pyrrhus under guard and with a message that they scorned to gain a victory through treason.

Pyrrhus, to show his gratitude, then sent back to Rome all the prisoners whom he held, without asking any ransom. This made the enemies friends, and a truce was concluded. It was one of the terms of the truce that Pyrrhus should leave Italy.

A large number of Greeks lived in Sicily. They had built Syracuse and other large cities and towns. At that time Carthage in Africa was a powerful city and the Carthaginians were trying to conquer the Sicilian Greeks. Pyrrhus crossed to Sicily to help his countrymen.

But his Italian friends got into trouble with the Romans again and begged him once more to help them. Accordingly he left Sicily and went back to Italy. Now, however, his good fortune forsook him. He was totally defeated by the Romans under Curius Dentatus and forced to leave Italy.

He now returned to Epirus, but as he was no lover of peace he soon went to war a second time with Macedonia. Again he conquered the land of Alexander, but again the king of Macedonia regained the kingdom.

Not content to rule Epirus, Pyrrhus next went into the Peloponnesus and fought against the Spartans, but they drove him from their territory.

Finally he went to Argos and took part in a civil war which was going on in that state.

A fight took place in one of the streets of Argos, and during it a woman threw a tile from the roof of her house. It struck Pyrrhus upon the head and stunned him, and some of the soldiers of the party against whom he was fighting ran up and killed him. (B.C.)

PART II

SICILY, about whose struggle with the Carthaginians you have just read, was the home of a famous mathematician named Archimedes. He was born at Syracuse in B.C., and was only a boy when Pyrrhus was in Sicily helping the Carthaginians fight the Sicilians. Many years later Syracuse was besieged by another enemy, the Romans. Archimedes, then an old man, proved of great help to his countrymen. He invented engines for throwing stones at the enemy. By using these engines the Sicilians kept the Romans at bay for a long time.

THE DEATH OF ARCHIMEDES

It is said that Archimedes set fire to the Roman ships with powerful burning-glasses. At last, howe

ver, Syracuse fell, and Archimedes was put to death by a Roman soldier, contrary to the order of the Roman commander.

Chapter 31

Cleomenes III

ABOUT a hundred years after the death of Alexander the Great lived a young prince named Cleomenes. His father was one of the kings of Sparta and bore the name of one of the greatest of Greek heroes, Leonidas, the famous defender of Thermopylae. One day, when the prince was about eighteen years old, he started from home to go hunting. He had not gone far from the city gate when one of his father's slaves overtook him and handed to him a writing tablet. On its waxed surface Cleomenes read the words, "Leonidas the king to Cleomenes: Come back to the palace the moment you have read this note." Cleomemes turned and went back toward the city.

Late in the afternoon he reached the palace. The gateway was hung with a garland of flowers, and entering he found the women busily arranging roses and lilies in every room.

As soon as he saw his father, he asked, "Is anyone going to be married?"

"You are," replied his father. "This evening I wish you to marry Agiatis, the widow of King Agis. I am having the palace decorated for the wedding. She is beautiful and good and the heiress of one of the richest men in Sparta."

"But," said Cleomenes, "how can she ever be willing to marry your son?"

"I am the king," replied Leonidas, "and she is bound to obey me."

"Since you wish it, I will marry her," said Cleomenes, "but I never can hope that she will love me."

Cleomenes had good reason for saying this; for Leonidas had caused his fellow-king, Agis, the husband of Agiatis, to be murdered.

Agis had been one of the best and greatest of Sparta's kings. He had been distressed at the state of his country when he came to the throne. The old customs of Lycurgus had been set aside. Since the close of the Peloponnesian War, when Sparta had proved more than a match for Athens, a great change had come over the kingdom. Her men were no longer warriors. The hope of Agis was that he might persuade the people to live according to the old laws which no one now obeyed.

But Leonidas, his fellow-king, did not wish to return to the old ways of living, and the five ephors, or magistrates of Sparta, were friends of his. They determined to put Agis to death. The ephors seized him upon the street and carried him to prison, and—for no other reason than that he had tried to carry out the laws of Lycurgus and restore the glory of Sparta—he was put to death.

THE RACE-COURSE OF SPARTA

This had been done at the order of Leonidas. Cleomenes therefore had reason to think that Agiatis never would marry him. However, the marriage took place as Leonidas wished, and although Agiatis hated Leonidas, who had murdered her husband, she soon learned to love Cleomenes, who was manly and true, and who devoted his life to making her happy.

She talked to him of Agis and what he had wished to do for Sparta. As Cleomenes listened he made up his mind to do just what Agis had wished to do. He saw that luxurious ways of living had weakened Sparta and destroyed her influence. And he saw also that his father's friends were not the few good and brave men still left in Sparta, but rich men who cared for nothing but money and pleasure.

PART II

LEONIDAS died a few years after the murder of Agis, and then Cleomenes became king.

At this time a great general named Aratus was at the head of a league of Greek cities called the Achæan League. It seemed likely that it would soon control all the Peloponnesus. Cleomenes therefore persuaded the Spartans to go to war against the Achæans.

In several battles he defeated Aratus and won for himself great fame as a soldier. This made the Spartans very fond of him, and he thought that the time had arrived when he might persuade them to obey once more the old laws and customs.

But the ephors were opposed to the changes which he wished to make, and so he boldly put them to death.

Next day he banished eighty citizens who were opposed to his plans. He then explained to the people why he had done this and why he had put the ephors to death.

"If without bloodshed," he said, "I could have driven from Sparta luxury and extravagance, debts and usury—the riches of the few and the poverty of the many—I should have thought myself the happiest of kings."

He declared that the laws of Lycurgus must be enforced and the land be again divided among the citizens.

The people were delighted when they heard all this, and much more were they pleased when Cleom- enes and his father-in-law were the first to give up their lands for division. The rest of the citizens did the same, and so, six hundred years after Lycurgus, there was a new division of property, and once more every Spartan had land enough to raise wheat and oil and wine for his family for a year.

Again the citizens dined at public tables on simple Spartan fare, and the youths were trained and drilled as Lycurgus had ordered. The Pyrrhic Dance, which trained soldiers in quick movements, was revived. Again the army was well disciplined, and the soldiers of Sparta became, as long ago, the best among the Greeks. The king himself set his people an example of simple living.

PYRRHIC DANCE

Some of the Greeks had laughed when Cleomenes said he would tread in the steps of Lycurgus and Solon; but when they saw Sparta victorious on the battlefield and the city prosperous and happy once more they could not help admiring the man who had brought the change about.

But in time a dreadful disaster befell Cleomenes and Sparta. The Achæan League invited the Macedonian king Antigonus to bring an army to help them against Cleomenes, and in a single battle the Spartans lost almost everything that they had gained.

The other king, who was Cleomenes' own brother, was killed, and out of six thousand men whom he commanded only two hundred survived.

Cleomenes made his way to Sparta and advised the citizens to submit to the Macedonians, which they did, and the independence of Sparta was gone forever.

Cleomenes had hopes of getting help from Ptolemy, king of Egypt. So he sailed to that country, and he was promised assistance. But, unfortunately, Ptolemy died, and the next king made Cleomenes a prisoner because an enemy of the great Spartan had said that he was plotting against the Egyptian king. Cleomenes saw no way of escape and so put an end to his life.

He was one of the greatest men of the last days of Greece.

Chapter 32

The Fall of Greece

THE states of Greece tried again and again to throw off the Macedonian yoke. Unfortunately, however, they often quarreled with one another and were not united against Macedonia. For this reason the kings of that state kept their place as masters of Greece for another hundred years.

Then the Romans invaded the country, and in a battle fought near a town called Pydna the Macedonians were defeated and their king Perseus was taken prisoner. This brought the Macedonian kingdom to an end. Macedonia was made part of the Roman Empire and men were sent from Rome to rule it.

Epirus was next captured. A hundred and fifty thousand of its inhabitants were sold into slavery and the state was made a Roman province.

After the fall of Macedonia the other states of Greece still continued fighting with one another. So in about twenty years (B.C.) a Roman army was sent against them. A battle was fought near Corinth in which the Greeks were completely defeated.

Corinth at that time was one of the richest and most beautiful cities in the world. After the battle the Roman general let his soldiers enter the houses and take what they pleased. Pictures, marble statues and jewelry were taken and shipped to Rome. It is said that two of the rough Roman soldiers played a game of dice on one of the finest pictures,—so little did they value works of art. Two thousand of the men of Corinth were put to death by the Romans, and the women and children were made slaves. After the buildings of the city had been plundered they were set on fire.

LAST DAYS OF CORINTH

And now Athens, Thebes, Sparta and the other Greek states became, like Macedonia, parts of the Empire of Rome.

From the rule of Rome Greece passed, in the Middle Ages, under the rule of Turkey, and it was only about seventy-five years ago that she revolted from Turkey and became once more an independent country.

If ever you go to Greece, as thousands of people do, to visit the places where her great men lived, you will see little but ruins. The columns of the temples are broken, the stones of their walls lie scattered on the ground.

RUINS OF THE ACROPOLIS AND TEMPLE OF THESEUS

And yet Greece, even amid ruin and decay, is still teaching the world. Many of the words that stand for branches of learning in our language to-day are Greek words. Such words are arithmetic and mathematics. They show plainly that the first teachers of mathematics in Europe were Greeks. Gymnasium and athletics are also Greek words. They show that the Greeks set us the example of running races, wrestling, jumping, throwing quoits and doing other such things to make our bodies strong. Poet, too, and poem are Greek, and remind us that the Greeks taught us how to write poetry. Grammar, rhetoric and geography are Greek words. So are logic, astronomy and surgery. These and hundreds of other words in daily use show how much we have inherited from the Greeks.

RUINS OF THE PARTHENON

Although the old-time glory of Greece has waned, the light of art and science which she kindled in the world grows brighter as time rolls on.

Made in the USA
Lexington, KY
31 December 2009